Perfect Psychometric Test Results

Kenexa® is a global human capital management firm which helps organizations recruit and retain talented people. Kenexa solutions include a wide range of psychometric and skills assessments, applicant tracking, employment process outsourcing, phone screening, structured interviews, performance management, multi-rater feedback surveys, employee engagement surveys and HR Analytics.

The book's authors are all employees within the Kenexa Assessment practice, based in London. Between them they have over 50 years of experience designing and analysing psychometric assessments across a wide range of industry sectors and for a range of applications such as selection, development and career counselling.

This book was written by
Dr Joanna Moutafi, C. Psychol.
Ian Newcombe, C. Psychol., AFBPsS
Sean Keeley, C. Psychol.
Mark Abrahams, MSc
Sarah Mortenson, MSc
Dunstan Arthur, MSc

Other titles in the *Perfect* series

Perfect
Psychometric
Test Results

Joanna Moutafi
Ian Newcombe
Sean Keeley
Mark Abrahams
Sarah Mortenson
Dunstan Arthur

BOOKS

Published by Random House Books 2007

2 4 6 8 10 9 7 5 3 1

Copyright © Kenexa 2005

First published in the United Kingdom in 2007 by
Random House Books

Random House Books
Random House, 20 Vauxhall Bridge Road,
London SW1V 2SA

www.randomhouse.co.uk

Addresses for companies within The Random House Group Limited
can be found at: www.randomhouse.co.uk/offices.htm

The Random House Group Limited Reg. No. 954009

A CIP catalogue record for this book
is available from the British Library

ISBN 9781905211678

The Random House Group Limited makes every effort to ensure that the
papers used in its books are made from trees that have been legally sourced
from well-managed and credibly certified forests. Our paper procurement
policy can be found at: www.randomhouse.co.uk/paper.htm

Typeset by Palimpsest Book Production Limited, Grangemouth, Stirlingshire
Printed in the UK by CPI Bookmarque, Croydon, CR0 4TD

Contents

Preface

If you are looking at this book you have probably been asked to take a psychometric test, perhaps as part of the recruitment process for a new job or perhaps as part of your company's internal training scheme. I have no doubt that you want to do your best, and the good news is that this book is specifically designed to help you. It contains everything you need to pass psychometric tests with flying colours.

The first section describes everything you need to know about what psychometric tests are and how you take them. It explains the different types of test and the sorts of conditions you should expect when the day comes. It also includes a section on online testing, which is being used more and more frequently. The next section gives you plenty of hints and tips about how to improve your performance, with advice on everything from calming your nerves to whether you should guess the answers. Finally, there are over 400 questions written by the expert team at Kenexa so that you can practise your skills and get used to the sorts of challenges you will face.

Once you have read this book you will:

- Understand much more about psychometric tests.
- Have a toolkit of techniques to help you through the process, from the moment you are invited to take a test to the testing day itself.
- Have an in-depth knowledge of the key types of questions that form psychometric tests.
- Have the confidence to complete any test to the best of your ability.

Psychometric tests are being used increasingly widely by employers, but with a bit of background knowledge and some practice, there is no reason you shouldn't perform to the very best of your abilities.

1 Introduction to psychometric tests

What are psychometric tests?

Let's start at the beginning. What does the word psychometric really mean? It is derived from the Greek words *psyche*, meaning 'soul', and *metron*, meaning to 'measure'. Strictly speaking, therefore, you might say that psychometric tests are tests that measure the soul, but in plain English, psychometric tests are instruments that measure in a structured way some characteristic of a person's ability or behaviour.

Types of psychometric test

There are two broad categories of psychometric test: tests of maximum performance and tests of typical performance. Organizations may use either or both categories of tests for selection decisions, as well as for employee development purposes, depending on the nature of the job. But of the different types of tests, the vast majority of organizations use two types: ability tests and personality questionnaires.

Tests of maximum performance

Tests of maximum performance are designed to measure the best performance that an individual can achieve in given circumstances. These are usually timed, and have right and wrong answers. Tests of maximum performance include ability tests and attainment tests.

Ability tests

For selection purposes, the most frequently used tests of maximum performance are ability tests. These can be tests of general mental ability, sometimes know as IQ tests, or of specific abilities, such as your ability in numerical, verbal, abstract or spatial reasoning. The main focus of this book is on the types of ability tests that you are most most likely to come across in your working life, and these are numerical reasoning tests, verbal reasoning tests and abstract reasoning tests.

Attainment tests

Attainment tests measure learning rather than ability. They can be on the same topic as ability tests – for example, some numerical tests are ability tests, and some numerical tests are attainment tests. These two types of tests are linked by the fact that ability is required for learning, and some learning is required for ability.

The main difference between attainment and ability tests is the way they are used. Ability tests are used to indicate what a person is capable of achieving in the future, whereas attainment tests are used to indicate what a person has learned and can do now. As a result, organizations are more likely to use ability tests than attainment tests for selection.

Tests of typical performance

Tests of typical performance are designed to measure how an individual would typically behave in given circumstances. They usually take the form of self-report questionnaires, which means that they ask you to report how you see yourself. More often than not they won't be timed, and they don't have right or wrong answers. Tests of typical performance include personality questionnaires, interest inventories and motivation questionnaires.

Personality questionnaires

In staff selection and development the most frequently used type of typical performance psychometric test is the personality questionnaire.

There are no right or wrong answers, which is why it is called a questionnaire rather than a test. It may seem a bit strange that people are expecting a questionnaire to assess something as complex as personality, but people have certain basic characteristics in common, and personality questionnaires are designed to assess someone's preferences, tendencies and behaviour with respect to these characteristics.

Interest inventories

Interest inventories are questionnaires that measure a person's interest in a specific occupation. Then questions typically draw together various combinations of occupation so that the person taking the test can choose the one they would find most interesting. These inventories then rank the occupations in order of preference. You might remember taking part in this sort of test at school in your careers sessions. The tests can be really useful in helping you find a direction for your career, and there's a great one on the BBC website, http://www.bbc.co.uk/science/humanbody/mind/surveys/careers/. However, because they are rarely used by employers, I won't be talking about them in this book. The only advice I would give is that you will get the most out of them if you are honest with yourself.

Motivation questionnaires

Motivation questionnaires are designed to measure the factors that motivate people at work. They typically consist of statements or questions to which you have to respond by specifying how much you agree or disagree with them. Again, they are most useful as a tool to help you get to know yourself, and the only relevant advice is to answer truthfully.

Why are psychometric tests used?

We have considered the different sorts of test that are available but have not yet answered the burning question: why do we have to sit them? What can psychometric tests tell an employer about a job applicant or an employee that a CV, a reference or an interview cannot?

The short answer is, 'quite a lot'. At the recruitment stage it can be difficult to form a clear idea of how a candidate will perform in a job, and when recruiters respond to CVs, references and interviews they inevitably do so on a personal level. It can be extremely helpful to have more objective information about a candidate's abilities, and research has shown that psychometric tests are the best predictors of how a candidate will perform. Not only do psychometric tests provide recruiters with more information than a CV, a reference and an interview can contain, they also provide more relevant information, which is more likely to help them make the right decision.

How can you be sure the tests are fair?

Perhaps you're still a bit sceptical and aren't convinced that these tests can actually measure a person's ability or personality. To put your mind at test I can assure you that every test that you will be asked to take should have gone through rigorous testing itself to make sure that it is both reliable and valid.

Reliability

A test is said to be reliable if it provides consistent measurement. It is important that someone taking the test on more than one occasion would get more or less the same score every time. If the results differed too much from one occasion to the next, it would be impossible to trust the future results of the test, and you would have to dismiss it as unreliable.

Validity

A test is said to be valid if it actually measures the thing it is intended to measure. A numerical test is valid, therefore, if it actually measures a person's numerical ability. Similarly, a personality questionnaire is valid if it actually assesses a person's personality.

But how do you check that a test actually measures someone's ability? The best way to do this is to follow someone who has taken the test and see if their abilities were predicted accurately. Unsurprisingly, over the years a lot of studies have followed people who got high scores in recruitment psychometric tests and compared them to those who got low scores. There is now a consistent body of evidence that shows that for many jobs, psychometric tests are the best single predictor of job performance – better than references, better than your performance in an interview, better even than your educational qualifications.

Obviously, tests cannot predict everything – people are much more complex than that. However, if you think about how expensive the recruitment process can be, how difficult it sometimes is to find the right people and how important it is that they stay, you can see why companies and organizations want to reduce the risk of recruitment in this practical and effective way.

This is not to say that all tests work for all jobs. In general, however, if a well-designed test has been appropriately selected on the basis of its relevance to a job it is likely to predict subsequent job performance.

There is no legal requirement for a test to have a certain level of reliability or validity, but organizations would avoid using tests for which there was no evidence of reliability or validity. After all, why would they spend money on a test that did not predict job performance? Exact details about how reliability and validity are measured are too involved to discuss here, but if you are interested in reading about this further a good introductory book would be *Reliability and Validity Assessment*, by Edward Carmines and Richard Zeller.

The main reason for mentioning reliability and validity is so that you can have a better understanding of what psychometric tests are. It's worth bearing in mind that your attitude towards the tests you take can affect your performance. If, for example, you believe that someone simply made up a few annoying questions that you now have to answer to get the job you want, you might be distracted and even frustrated while you are completing the test, and this will affect your performance. If, on the other hand, you understand that there is a scientific approach behind the construction of psychometric tests, you might have a more positive attitude when taking the test, and having a positive attitude towards the test will make it more likely that you will perform at your best.

Do psychometric tests discriminate?

The short answer is, 'yes, they do discriminate'. But this is precisely what they are designed to do. They discriminate between people who have a good or a bad head for numbers, who are extroverted or introverted, who are able or not able to think in the abstract and so on. Discrimination may sound like a negative word, but it really means identifying the differences between people, which is what every employer needs to do in order to find the right person for the job. The more important question is: do psychometric tests discriminate unfairly?

Unfair discrimination

Every employer wants to choose the person who is most suitable for the role. Fair discrimination occurs when employers choose someone whose personal characteristics and abilities are well suited to the job requirements. Unfair discrimination is when they employ – or do not employ – someone by considering personal characteristics and abilities that are irrelevant to the job requirements. Unfair discrimination can be either direct or indirect.

Direct discrimination
Direct discrimination happens when an organization does not employ an individual because of a characteristic that is irrelevant to the job, such as gender or race, and it is usually illegal. There are five main acts that regulate equal opportunities in selection:

- Sex Discrimination Act 1986
- Race Relations Act 1976
- Disability Discrimination Act 1995
- Employment Equality Regulations 2003
- Age Discrimination Act 2006

Indirect discrimination

Indirect discrimination occurs when an organization does not employ an individual because of a characteristic that indirectly causes discrimination against a group of people. For example, if a company selected individuals for positions in the accounts department according to their height, this could indirectly discriminate against women, who are typically shorter than men. Such unjustified discrimination can also be illegal.

However, indirect discrimination that is justified can be acceptable. For example, if the position was not in the accounts department but in a basketball team, selecting individuals by height could be justified. Therefore, companies should discriminate among individuals only on the basis of characteristics that are relevant to the job requirements.

How are tests scored?

Ability tests

Ability tests are typically scored according to the number of questions answered correctly. Some tests use the simple rule of the total score being the number of correct answers. So if you answer 15 questions correctly in a 20-question test, your score will be 15. Other tests use more complex procedures to arrive at a score. As well as the number of correct answers, they will also consider things such as whether the questions answered correctly were easy or difficult, whether you could have guessed the answer and so on.

It's important to remember that ability tests are not always scored by considering just one aspect – whether each question was answered correctly or incorrectly. Scores are occasionally based on other factors, such as the total number of questions that were attempted, the number of mistakes made, how long it took to complete each question or the whole test, or perhaps a combination of these factors.

The fact is that you cannot be sure how the test you have to take will be scored. But even if you were sure, the most important thing would be to get as many correct answers as you could. This is not only included in every formula or algorithm used to calculate your score, but it is also frequently the only measure used to derive your score.

Personality questionnaires

Personality questionnaires consist of a number of statements, questions or adjectives to which you have to respond according to how much you agree or disagree. You are typically given a multiple choice of answers – for example, the choices may be 'Strongly disagree', 'Disagree', 'Neutral', 'Agree' and 'Strongly agree'. You could be given more or fewer options, depending on what detail the recruiters want to get from your responses.

In-depth details about personality questionnaires and the structure of personality tests are given in Chapter 6, but here is an example that will give you an idea of how the questionnaires are scored.

One of the basic aspects of personality that is typically included in personality questionnaires is extroversion, and the questions that are designed to assess this aspect of personality will be scored on a scale, with the lower end of a scale indicating you are not at all extroverted, and the higher end indicating that you are very extroverted. In order to get your total score for extroversion, the individual scores of each question will be added up.

Say that there are five questions measuring extroversion, and each is scored on a scale of 1–5 – that is you receive 1 point if you choose option A, 2 points for option B, 3 points for option C and so on. If you are extremely introverted, your responses to each of the five questions will correspond to a 1 score, so your total score on extroversion will be $1+1+1+1+1=5$. If, on the other hand, you are extremely extroverted, your responses to each of the five questions will correspond to a 5 score, so your total score on extroversion will be $5+5+5+5+5=25$.

What score do you need to pass?

Ability tests

In some ways it would be useful to know in advance how well you need to do in order to pass an ability test. If you discover that the pass mark is low, your confidence will probably go up when you are taking the test. Conversely, finding out that the pass mark is quite high will probably increase your anxiety. The best thing you can do is focus on your performance and try not to worry about your score. You should remember that recruiters are generally not trying to select people with the highest abilities, but to deselect those with the lowest abilities. As a rule, organizations typically reject no more than about 30 per cent of applicants on the basis of any one psychometric test. However, if you are applying for a job where the ability test is extremely relevant – if you want to be an accountant, for example, and have to pass a numerical test – you will need to get a good mark.

Personality questionnaires

We already know that personality questions have no right or wrong answers, so you would be forgiven for wondering how on earth you can pass. This is a hard question because there are so many factors involved in determining the result of these tests that it would be difficult to summarize them all. If we look at it from the recruiter's point of view, however, things become a little clearer. Recruiters are looking for somebody to fit a role, and they will probably have an idea of the sort of qualities they want. For example, good sales people score quite highly on extroversion, influence and persuasiveness scales, so recruiters will be likely to look for similarly high scores from the candidates for such positions.

In order to put together an idea of the qualities that will be suitable for a role, recruiters and test providers carry out an in-depth job analysis. This helps them develop a picture of what they are looking for, but it's only the first step. The next will be to assess how many people have applied and decide how many will need to be deselected. For example, if they want to sift out a large number of candidates, their selection decisions will be more stringent. Again, it is difficult to predict what recruiters are looking for, so the best thing you can do is simply concentrate on giving the answers that feel right to you.

What do test scores mean?

Ability scores

Let us go back to the example of the ability test for which your score was 15. What does that mean to you about your ability? Probably not much, and it doesn't mean much to the recruiters either! For your score to have any meaning, the recruiters will need to compare it with a large group of people who have completed the same test. For this reason, when you receive feedback on your results, you will not generally receive your actual test score, but a percentile score or a grade.

A percentile is a number between 1 and 100, and it shows what percentage of the people who completed the same test got a lower score than you did. Therefore, if your score, 15, corresponds to the 60th percentile, it means that your score of 15 was better than the score achieved by 60 per cent of the people who took the test.

A grade is a simplified version of the percentile system. Grade A is achieved by the top 10 per cent of scorers, grade B by the next 20 per cent of scorers, grade C by the middle 40 per cent of scorers, grade D by the next 20 per cent of scorers, and grade E by the bottom 10 per cent of scorers.

Even though it's normally only the bottom 30 per cent who will not get through, you should bear in mind that you are not being compared with a random group of people but with a group that broadly corresponds to the sort of people who will apply for the job you are after. Unfortunately, you can only guess at the scores they might get, so the best thing you can do is forget the pass mark altogether and do the best you can.

Personality scores

What about personality scores? Let us say that you received neither 5 nor 25 in extroversion, but a score of 20. What would that mean? The answer is the same as it was for the ability score: on its own, the score doesn't say very much. You need something to compare it with, and as with ability scores, your personality questionnaire scores will be compared with those of a large group of people.

Unlike ability scores, however, the percentage of people who scored lower than you is not important. What is important is whether your score indicates that you are 'not at all', 'a little', 'a lot' or 'extremely' extroverted compared to the rest of the group. People are grouped into broad categories so that employers can get a broad sense of their personality. There are quite a few of these categories, and they are controlled by a number of factors, but it is important to emphasize that scores for ability tests and for personality questionnaires are interpreted with different levels of precision.

Can practice improve your score?

Ability tests

When it comes to ability tests, the simple answer is 'yes'. The reason I am writing this book and you are reading it is because there are definite advantages to be gained from knowing more about psychometric tests, and those advantages will lead to better scores. You can definitely improve your score to a certain extent, but the important question is, by how much can you improve your score.

Let us look at an extreme example to answer this question. If Albert Einstein had taken an ability test, how would he have performed? It is hard to be certain, but you would expect him to have scored pretty highly. Imagine if he had had a different background, however. Rather than having been educated in Germany, where there were good schools and universities, what would have happened if he had been brought up in a remote place and received no formal education? How would he have performed if he had completed an ability test in these circumstances? Probably not so well.

Now imagine someone who is not naturally very intelligent. How would that person perform in an ability test? Probably quite poorly. But what if this person were given the opportunity to practise lots of ability test questions and to get used to the forms they took and the sorts of things they were looking for? How would this affect the scores? They would probably still be pretty poor, but they would be at the top of the range of scores that not-so-intellgent candidates could expect to achieve.

Practising ability tests will not make you smarter than you are, because our potential for intelligence is something we are born with. This may sound unfair, but it is just as fair as everything else in life. People are born with differences in all kinds of respects: some will be good at playing the piano, some will be good at acting, some will be good at dancing. But what might have happened if Nureyev had never taken ballet lessons and participated in a ballet competition? He would probably have failed, albeit very elegantly!

The fact remains that people have different potentials for intelligence, just as they have different potentials for everything else, but practice can make you realize your full potential and achieve your best possible performance in an ability test. This means that even if you are taking the same psychometric test as a person with higher ability than you, if you are familiar with the test and have practised and they have not, you may perform better than they do.

Personality questionnaires

Can you also improve your scores in a personality questionnaire? This question does not really make sense, because there are no right or wrong answers in personality questionnaires, so there is no such thing as a 'good' or a 'bad' score. The questionnaires are designed to get a picture of what you are like so that they can match this to the job requirements. If you are not honest in your answers, you could end up in a job that really doesn't suit you. There are other issues relating to personality questionnaires that you should be aware of, and these are discussed in Chapter 6.

What will the testing procedure be like?

If you are invited to complete a psychometric test you may have to go into the office or to a specialist testing centre. Alternatively, you could be invited to complete a test online, and we will consider this in more detail in the following section.

Ability tests are administered under examination conditions. You will typically be taking the test as part of a group of between 10 and 30 people. There will be an administrator, who will begin by explaining the procedure in detail, probably by reading a script. This script may sound a little unnatural, but it is used to make sure that participants in different sessions receive the same information. After the procedure is explained, the administrator will read the test instructions. Listen very carefully to the instructions. If you are in doubt about anything the administrator says, make sure you ask before the session begins, because once the session has started, the administrator will not be allowed to answer any questions.

The session will be timed, and when the time is up you will be asked to stop writing. You may receive a warning 5 minutes or 1 minute before the time is up, but this will vary from test to test. Administrators are very strict with timing to make sure that no participant has an unfair advantage. It is a good idea to wear a watch and to keep track of the time, so that you can finish as many questions as possible.

Personality questionnaires are administered under less stringent conditions. Because these are not tests of maximal performance and are not timed, the main concern will be for you to be comfortable and not distracted by anything. As with the ability tests, you will receive instructions, but there will be no time limit for you to complete the test. Do not waste your time, however, because if everyone else finishes before you, you could get distracted.

What are online tests?

Online tests are psychometric tests that are completed on a computer and are accessed through the internet. More and more employers are taking this option, because it is much easier to organize. Not going into a testing session and not being supervised while you take the test have advantages, including the facts that you will be taking the test at home and in your own time. You can make yourself as comfortable as you like and choose a time when you will perform at your best.

Differences between online and offline tests

Even though online and offline tests are considered to be equivalent, there are differences between the two:

- The conditions under which you complete the tests are different.
- You won't be able to ask any questions.
- There is typically only one version of an offline test, so all applicants complete the same version whereas there are several equivalent versions of an online test.
- Online tests may be affected by your PC capabilities and internet connection.

Creating the best testing conditions

When you take a normal psychometric test at a testing site, you have no control over the conditions because they are standardized. When you take an online test, however, you can create your own conditions. Ideally, of course, you want to set up the sorts of conditions that will help you perform to the best of your ability. This is what you should do.

- Chose to complete the test at the time of day when you are usually most alert. For most people, this will be during the morning.

- Try to make sure that nothing will distract you. Ask people who are at home with you not to disturb you, turn off your phone, sign out of your email and messenger accounts, and turn off any music or appliances that create white noise in the background.
- Try to make sure that the room temperature is neither too high nor to low. A slightly cooler temperature may help you maintain alertness.
- Make sure the room is well lit.
- Wear comfortable clothing.
- Make sure that you have any equipment that you might need, such as paper and pencil and a calculator.
- Do not drink, eat or smoke during the test. This will distract you and waste valuable time.
- Remember that ability tests are timed, and when you are doing online tests you will not be warned when your time is running out. There will typically be a countdown clock on your screen while you are taking the test. You should occasionally check this, but not so often that you lose your concentration.

What if I have a question when I am taking an online test?

Although there is no administrator who can answer your questions when you are completing a test online, you do have the advantage of being able to go through the instructions for as long as you require before you start the test. Bear in mind that the test setters know that you won't be able to ask anyone for clarification if you don't understand anything, and they will have gone to great lengths to present the instructions in so much detail that you shouldn't need to ask any questions. If you really don't understand something crucial, you could contact the person who asked you to complete the test. This should be your last resort, however, because showing that you are unable to understand very detailed instructions might not give the best impression. If you really are stumped, remember that the issue you're unsure about may well become obvious as you start to take the test.

How do online test setters make sure people don't cheat?

Online tests will have a time limit, but this wouldn't stop someone from cheating if they really wanted to. One measure that is often employed is to create different versions of the test. There are two ways of making a new version of a test. The first is to create a parallel form; the second is to derive each new test from one bank of items (questions).

Parallel forms

Parallel forms of a test are different tests that have an equal number of questions, with each test having the same properties as any other test. This means that all the versions have the same reliability and validity, and they are designed so that a person will receive a similar score no matter which version they complete.

Item banks

Item-banked tests are created out of a large bank of questions (items) with known properties. Because the properties of each question are known, they can be compared with each other and grouped into equivalent tests. This means that two item-banked versions of a test will have an equal number of questions, and each question in the first test will have equivalent properties to its corresponding question in the second test. Rather than just having equivalent tests, therefore, item-banked tests also have equivalent questions.

Because the properties of each question are known, all the questions with the same properties can be used interchangeably in any version of the test, and when you are creating a test, you have more combinations of questions that you can use. This means that the probability of a candidate receiving the same test as someone else is very low. So item-banked tests are used in order to reduce the chances of cheating.

Item-banked tests are created through a sophisticated statistical procedure called Item Response Theory, which is far beyond the scope of this book, but if you are interested in reading about this further, a good introductory read would be *Fundamentals of Item Response Theory* by Ronald Hambleton, H. Swaminathan and H. Jane Rogers.

Technical considerations

Online tests are inevitably affected by the state of your computer and internet connection, so you must make sure that you will have no problems while you are taking the test.

PC specifications

When you are asked to complete an online test you will be sent an invitation. Remember to read this carefully, because it will probably include details of the PC specifications that are necessary for the test to run properly. You should check that your PC's specifications match those required before you take the test. Alternatively, some tests have an in-built mechanism that automatically checks whether the PC specifications are met and will not allow you to take the test if they are not.

If you experience such a problem, you should contact the person who sent you the invitation to complete the test. You might be experiencing problems because of a setting in your computer, in which case they should be able to talk you through it. Alternatively, if your PC does not meet the required specifications, you will have to complete the test from a different PC.

Internet requirements

The internet connection requirements will be specified with the PC specifications. Test developers are, of course, aware that you may be using a computer that is old or slow, and that your internet connection may not be very fast. Online tests are, therefore, generally designed to be accessible by at least 99 per cent of users. If you do encounter a problem with accessing the test or while taking the test, contact the person who sent you the invitation and they should be able to help you.

At this point I must warn you about something so that you don't fall into a not-so-uncommon trap. If you start taking the test but want to stop halfway through, don't just turn off your computer or close the window and then pretend that the internet connection was interrupted or that your PC crashed. It is easy for most test programmers to track your signal back and work out what caused your test to shut down, so you won't fool anyone. The golden rule is: start the test only when you feel ready to do so, because you are unlikely to be able to quit a test once you have started it.

What if I can't get online?

If you do not have a PC or an internet connection, it's not the best idea to get back to the recruiter to ask what alternatives there are. Performing well in a job means overcoming simple problems, and there are enough PCs in public spaces, such as libraries and internet cafés, for you to be able to find a solution. If you have the opportunity, I would recommend trying to use a friend's computer, which will give you more control over your environment while you are taking the test.

Points to consider

Do you have a disability?

The Disability Discrimination Act prevents employers from directly discriminating against applicants on the basis of their disability. If you have some form of disability, therefore, you are protected from discrimination. But what happens if you have a disability that interferes with your performance on a psychometric test? If this is the case, arrangements can usually be made for you to complete the test in a different format.

For example, if you have a motor disability and cannot easily get to the testing centre, you might be able to complete the test from somewhere else, possibly even your home. If you have a disability that interferes with your ability to use a keyboard you might be able to complete the test in a paper-and-pencil format. If you have a visual or hearing impairment, arrangements could be made for you to take the test in an alternative form. If you have a disability such as dyslexia, you might be allocated extra time to complete the test.

Because alternative arrangements will have to be made, it's a good idea to give the recruiters plenty of notice.

Is English your first language?

If you are applying for a job in an English-speaking country, it is possible that you will be expected to take a test in English, even if it is not your first language. In general, if the role requires a good use of English, you will probably not be given an opportunity to complete the test in a language other than English. However, you should let the administrator know that you are not answering in your first language. It is important that the information gets through to the recruiters so that they can bear it in mind during the decision-making process.

Will the fact that English is your second language affect your test scores? I am afraid that this will depend on your fluency, but most tests don't use particularly complex or unusual vocabulary. Some tests will expect you to read material quickly, but if you have a good level of fluency and have put in the practice you should be able to deal with this challenge.

The fact that English is not your first language is unlikely to affect your score on abstract reasoning tests, because the only wording these tests have are the initial instructions. If you have any questions about the instructions make sure you ask them before the testing session begins.

A lack of fluency in English should not affect your results in numerical tests because the questions typically use very simple wording to make sure that the test measures numerical ability only and not reading comprehension.

If you have to take a verbal reasoning test your results might depend on the test and on your fluency. If you are applying for a job that requires fluent English – such as a journalist – the need for fluency could be reflected in the test. However, when language fluency is an important aspect of the role, recruiters typically require specific language qualifications. Verbal tests are designed to test your reasoning ability in a verbal context, not necessarily your knowledge of the language.

Personality questionnaires typically include questions with simple terminology because their aim is to assess your personality, and it is essential that you do not misunderstand the questions. For this reason you are usually allowed to ask for clarification if you don't understand a question. Your fluency should not, therefore, be a major issue with personality questionnaires.

2 Improve your performance

The most significant way to improve your performance in psychometric tests is to find out how the questions work and to practise solving a few. There are, however, a few other changes you can make and tips you can learn that could make a difference. I've put together a quick-and-easy checklist of things to consider when you are preparing for your test.

Before the test

Familiarization and practice

Familiarizing yourself with psychometric tests is the first step to success. You will need to have a clear picture of what these tests are and which particular type of test you will be sitting. Make sure that you focus on the test or tests that are relevant to you. You will need to familiarize yourself with what the test will look like, what it will measure and what the testing conditions will be. Once all these are clear, you need to practise.

Try to make sure that you start working towards improving your performance a few days before your test date. This has two main benefits:

- Sleep is extremely good for your memory, and if you have the opportunity to get some sleep after learning something you'll notice it really helps it lodge in your memory.
- You need to give yourself enough time to see the improvement in your scores. This will boost your confidence and make sure your anxiety remains under control during the test.

Anxiety

Anxiety affects different people in different ways. Some people get extremely nervous under test conditions, and so they make mistakes. Others find that a bit of nervous energy really gets them going and slightly improves their performance. Still others seem able to look completely relaxed throughout the process, even though it's quite likely they are hiding their nerves. So what is it about psychometric tests that makes us feel nervous? To begin with, the tests have important consequences. Whether or not you get a job could depend on the results you achieve. Equally, not knowing exactly what questions will come up can be nerve-racking. And finally, the thought that you are going to be judged by your answers might be a cause for concern: few of us like being judged, and no one likes to fail.

So what can you do to reduce your anxiety? This really depends on the sort of person you are, but there are a couple of techniques that I often recommend:

- Rationalize your thoughts.
- Do some simple exercises.

Rationalize your thoughts

A good way to take the edge off your anxiety is to think logically about the things that make you anxious. You may, for example, be anxious because you don't know exactly what questions will come up. However, you should bear in mind that you do know that the questions will be structured in a certain way, and if you go through all the practice questions in this book, you will have worked with enough examples to have a good idea of what's coming up. The wording of the questions will be different, but the underlying logic will be the same. So there's nothing to worry about: you will have practised the thought processes required to solve all the different types of question, and this will make it easy to solve the questions, even if they have different wording.

Perhaps the root of your worry lies in the idea that you are being judged and that you have to get everything right so you don't come across as stupid. If this is the case, it might help to put things into perspective. When it comes to being judged, you should remember that the test will probably be marked by a computer or by a psychometric testing professional who will have seen hundreds, if not thousands, of answer sheets. Your prospective employer will be interested in your overall scores, not whether you get one or two specific questions right or wrong, so you needn't worry about a silly mistake coming back to haunt you.

The major source of concern for most people will be the consequences of the test. What happens if you don't do well enough to get the job? Again, a bit of perspective can help. You might really want the job: perhaps it seems perfect for you or it sounds like a once-in-a-lifetime opportunity. The truth is, there is no such thing as a perfect job. Every job has its pros and cons, and before you start work there is no way of telling if the job will suit you. How can you tell if you will get on with your boss or with your new colleagues? Will you be able to handle the workload? And as for once-in-a-lifetime opportunities, who can tell what's round the corner? There may be an even better job on the horizon – you just have to keep looking for it.

One thing you should bear in mind is that if you are not the right person for the job, it probably means the job is not the right one for you. It may seem hard, but if the recruiters decide not to give you the job, it's probably for very good reasons. After all, there's no point wasting your time in a job that you don't enjoy and that you find hard to handle because it requires different skills from the ones you have. It would be much better to find a job that you'll be good at because you have the right skills and abilities. So, prepare for the test and do your best, but remember that this is not the most important moment in your life!

Do relaxation exercises

If rationalizing your anxieties doesn't work for you, it might help to learn a few simple relaxation exercises. There is a useful one with the rather grand name the 'progressive muscular relaxation technique'. All you need to do is concentrate on one set of muscles at a time – for example, your toes, followed by your feet, followed by your calves and so on – and tense each group of muscles for a few seconds before relaxing them to their original state, and then relaxing them even more until you are as relaxed as possible. Have you noticed that when you are a bit stressed your shoulders start to hunch? This can be a good way of reminding yourself how tense your muscles are and how relaxed they can be.

If you are interested in trying out different relaxation techniques, the easiest way to find them is on the web. Do a search for 'relaxation techniques', choose one and practise it a few times. Once you find one that works for you, you'll also be able to do it on the test day.

Even if you manage to rationalize your thoughts and perform the relaxation exercises, you may still feel some anxiety during the testing session. Don't let this alarm you: it's good for you. Research shows that small levels of anxiety actually help your performance. Anxiety keeps you alert and speeds up your mental processing.

The night before

Tiredness

I'm sure you have already been advised many times to get a good night's sleep before you take any exams. The same is true for psychometric tests, which are also designed to test your maximum performance. Remember to get a good night's sleep the night before a psychometric test, even if you feel that you need to practise more.

The benefit you will get from being rested and alert is much greater than the benefit you will get from a few hours of extra practice the night before. Moreover, if you come across a question that you can't solve, this is bound to increase your anxiety. The harm your anxiety will have on your performance is much greater than the benefit you will derive from learning to solve one particular item at this stage.

Mood

You may think this is not important, but many studies have shown that mood affects your performance. The rule is simple: being in a good mood can help your performance, whereas being in a bad mood can harm your performance. You can, of course, argue that your mood is not something you can alter so there is little point in mentioning it. Perhaps you cannot change your mood, but you can definitely make an effort to avoid circumstances that will get you into a bad mood, such as not discussing sensitive subjects on the day of the testing or the night before.

The testing day

If you are invited to complete a psychometric test in a testing place rather than completing it online, there are some basic things you should remember.

First, make sure that you arrive at the testing place in good time. If you arrive late, the administrators will not wait for you and you will miss the test. Even if they do allow you to complete the test at a later date, punctuality is important for every job, so this will give a bad first impression. Ideally, you should aim to arrive at the testing place about 20 minutes before the arranged time. This will allow you to be prepared for unexpected conditions, such as heavy traffic, and it will also allow you some time to concentrate and relax before the session begins. In addition, you will be dealing with your anxiety about the test itself right before the session, so you shouldn't add the extra stress of wondering if you will get there on time.

Make sure you have everything you need. Pens, pencils, a calculator, spectacles, your hearing aid – write a checklist before the day of the test and stick to it. Also, don't forget to take the invitation letter, your passport or any other documents you have been asked to bring along.

Finally, wear comfortable clothing. You have to minimize the things that will distract you during the test, so make sure your clothes are not going to cause you any discomfort.

The testing session

Asking questions

Some people seem to ask questions at every opportunity, while others hate speaking up so much that they'll ask a question only if they really can't manage without the answer. People who always ask questions are likely to be extroverted and confident, whereas people who tend to be a bit shyer might be introverted and self-critical. If you are shy, however, the testing session is one of those times when you have to get over this. If you have a question, no matter how uncomfortable this might make you feel, you have to ask it.

If there is anything you don't understand in the testing procedure or the test instructions, or if there's anything you need to change in the testing conditions – for example, if the air conditioning is blowing right at you and you would like to change your seat – just talk to the administrator. If you can't find the right time to do so, remember that the administrator will always ask if there are any questions before the test begins. Remember that the administrator will not be able to answer any questions about the instructions once the test has started. Make sure you deal with any practical issues, such as changing your seat, before the test begins, otherwise you will lose time and probably your concentration.

During the test

The most important things to do during the test are to stay calm and concentrate. However, you must also consider the following factors.

Most tests are in a multiple-choice format, and you will typically fill in your answers on an answer sheet rather than on the actual test. Remember to double-check that your answers correspond to the questions.

You must fill in your answers in the way that you have been instructed. If you have been asked to use a pencil, use a pencil; if you have been asked to put a line in the appropriate circle rather than filling it in, that is what you should do. Computers often score the tests automatically, and you must make sure that the computer will be able to read your answers.

If you can't decide between two responses, don't choose both. This will be marked as an incorrect response, even if one of your two choices is correct.

If you have no idea how to solve a question or if you find one difficult or confusing, go on to the next question. Your final score will depend on how many questions you answer, not on whether you have missed out a question. However, bear in mind that questions tend to get progressively harder as you go through the test. It's best to skip questions only if you think you can't solve them, not because you simply think they will take up a lot of time.

Guessing the answer

Should you make a guess if you cannot solve a question? Test administrators often get asked this question, but they always respond by saying either 'I'm sorry, I don't have that information' or 'I'm sorry, I can't give you that information.'

Unfortunately, I'm in the same position. Sometimes incorrect answers are scored with a negative point, sometimes they are just not scored, so it is not possible to say if it's worth taking a guess if you don't know the answer.

As a rule, if you are not sure about the correct answer, try to make your best guess, but try not to answer completely at random. For example, if you can rule out three of five available options, you might decide to make an educated guess about the correct one of the two remaining options. However, it's not a good idea to pick an answer at random if you can't eliminate any of the options.

After the test

After you have completed the test, you will probably want to forget all about it until you receive the results. It is, however, worth thinking about the types of question you found most difficult and the ones you were most unsure about. Ideally, you will have passed on to the next stage in the recruitment process and won't have to sit another test in the immediate future, but you never know when you might have to take another, and it's best to learn as much as you can from the one you've just passed. Psychometric tests are being used more and more frequently, and you should make sure that you are able to complete them to the best of your ability.

Feedback

Typically, you will receive your results a few days after the test. This could take the form of a simple notice telling you if you have passed on to the next stage of the recruitment process, or it could be a more detailed report showing, for example, where your score was in relation to the comparison group – that is, what percentage of the comparison group scored lower than you. A more detailed report could look like this:

> You recently completed a verbal ability test. This test is designed to provide a fair, objective, rapid and practical measure of your skills in evaluating verbal information, which are skills that are relevant in many managerial roles.
>
> To give meaning to your scores, they have been compared to a group of other managers. When interpreting the test scores it is important to remember that all scores are relative to this group. Remember also that while verbal ability is important for managers, it is only part of the picture. Many people have useful strategies to compensate for less well developed skills of verbal analysis. Your score is in the 60th percentile of the comparison group of managers. In other words, you performed at a level that was typical of most people in your comparison group.

If you don't receive any feedback on your test results, ask for it. Learning about your abilities will help in your development, irrespective of what happens with the specific job you applied for. If you completed a personality questionnaire you might also receive a summary of your profile. Take some time to consider whether you find it representative, whether you would have answered differently in some areas if you were to complete the questionnaire again, and whether there are areas you think you should work on. You can use this information to help with your personal development.

3 Numerical reasoning tests

Numerical reasoning tests assess your ability to reason with numerical information. They are typically found in two basic formats:

- A series of questions containing numerical information.
- Numerical data shown in a table, graph or a chart, followed by a series of questions linked to these data. Tests like this also assess your ability to extract numerical information when it is presented in different ways.

Companies use numerical reasoning tests in both formats, but the second type is the more common, especially if the tests are for graduate or managerial positions, because the ability to extract numerical information when it is presented in various ways is often required at these levels. No matter what the format, all the tests will expect you to have a basic knowledge of simple calculations, so we will start from there.

Simple calculations

Basic numerical calculations

Basic numerical calculations cover adding, subtracting, multiplying and dividing. Although it is unlikely that a question will require just these basic calculations, it is probable that you would need to use these as part of the solution. You will usually be able to use a calculator during the test, but remember that if you can do simple calculations in your head you will save yourself a lot of valuable time.

Following are a few examples to jog your memory on basic calculations. During the testing session you can perform the ones you are comfortable with in your head and use a calculator only for the ones you are less confident with.

Practice questions

For the practice questions that follow calculate the value that should replace the x. Remember that time will be important in the actual test, so you should start practising your speed as well as your accuracy. Try to solve the following examples as quickly as you can.

	QUESTION	ANSWER
1.	$14 + 9 = x$	
2.	$23 + 8 = x$	
3.	$32 + 27 = x$	
4.	$27 + x = 32$	
5.	$18 + x = 47$	
6.	$29 + x = 42$	
7.	$53 - 18 = x$	
8.	$27 - 16 = x$	
9.	$68 - 29 = x$	
10.	$7 \times 8 = x$	

11. $6 \times 9 = x$

   ....

12. $8 \times 9 = x$

   ....

13. $7 \times x = 42$

   ....

14. $4 \times x = 36$

   ....

15. $4 \times x = 52$

   ....

16. $36 \div 3 = x$

   ....

17. $63 \div 7 = x$

   ....

18. $45 \div 9 = x$

   ....

Rounding off answers

Rounding off numbers is something that you will probably not be asked to perform directly in a question, but it is something that you should be familiar with, as it is often required as part of a solution.

When to round up

Rounding up means that you should increase the required digit by a value of 1 and drop off the digits to its right. You need to round up if the number next to the required digit is 5, 6, 7, 8 or 9. For example, if you are required to round off 3.257 to two decimal places it will become 3.26.

When to round down

Rounding down means that you keep the required digit as it is but drop off the digits to its right. You need to round down if the number next to the required digit is 0, 1, 2, 3 or 4. For example, if you are required to round off 0.24 to one decimal place it will become 0.2.

Fill in the questions below to practise rounding off digits.

TIP: When you round off to a decimal that has more than one digit on its right, you should consider only the first digit that is on the right. For example, if you are required to round off 0.2349 to two decimal places it should become 0.23.

Practice questions

Round off the following numbers to 2 decimal places.

	QUESTION	ANSWER
19.	13.453	
20.	10.215	
21.	29.195	

Round off the following numbers to 1 decimal place.

	QUESTION	ANSWER
22.	35.881	
23.	1.025	
24.	2.2445	

Further numerical calculations

In addition to the basic numerical calculations, there are other types of calculation that you should be comfortable with when you take a numerical reasoning test, including averages, percentages, inverse percentages and ratios. These calculations are not only likely to be part of a question, but they will frequently be the question itself. We will consider each category in turn, and for each type of question you will be given the general solution and also the detailed solution for a specific example. You will then be presented with a number of examples to practise.

Averages

The average, or mean, of a number of values is simply the sum of the values divided by the number of values.

QUESTION: What is the average of A, B and C?
SOLUTION: Add the values together, and divide their total by the number of values.
FORMULA: $(A + B + C) \div Number\ of\ values$

SAMPLE QUESTION: What is the average of 5, 14, 8, 21 and 32?
SOLUTION: $(5 + 14 + 8 + 21 + 32) \div 5 = 16$, so the average of these numbers is 16.

In a similar type of question, you could be given the average and all but one of the values, and asked to calculate the missing value.

QUESTION: What is the value of A, if B = b, C = c, D = d, and the average of A, B, C and D is x?
SOLUTION: Multiply the average (x) by the number of values that make up the average (here the number of values is 4, since there are a, b, c and d). From this subtract the values that you are given (b, c, d). The remaining value is the value of A.
FORMULA: $(x \times number\ of\ values) - b - c - d$

> **SAMPLE QUESTION:** If the average of 1.2, 2.5, 3.6 and A is 3.5, what is the value of A?
> **SOLUTION:** You have to work out $(3.5 \times 4) - 1.2 - 2.5 - 3.6 = 14 - 1.2 - 2.5 - 3.6 = 3.7$, so the value of A is 3.7.

Now try the following examples on averages, rounding off your answers to one decimal place.

Practice questions

QUESTION	ANSWER

26. What is the average of 13, 16, 19 and 11?

27. What is the average of 450, 320 and 420?

28. What is the average of $^1/_5$, $^1/_6$ and $^1/_7$?

Sample questions

QUESTION	ANSWER

29. What was the average temperature in °C this summer, if the average monthly temperature was 15°C in June, 17°C in July and 18°C in August?

30. What is the height of a basketball player, if the average height in his team is 1.98 cm, and the heights of his four team players are 1.95, 1.94, 2.05 and 2.02 cm?

QUESTION	ANSWER
31. If the average 200 metres running time of five runners was 27.8 seconds, and the timings of the four runners were 23.5, 25.1, 29.8 and 30.2, what was the timing of the fifth runner?	

Percentages

A percentage is a way of expressing a number as a fraction of 100, so it is simply a number divided by 100. Therefore 5 per cent is the same as 5 ÷ 100 and also the same as 0.05. You must be familiar with these transformations because you will often need to transform a percentage, 5 per cent, into a decimal, 0.05, in order to make the calculations required for a numerical reasoning question and then transform the answer back into a percentage. The following examples will help you practise with these transformations and will also help you to practise further with rounding off decimals.

Practice questions

Transform the following percentages into decimals, rounding off your answer to 2 decimal places.

QUESTION	ANSWER
32. 13%	
33. 75.8%	
34. 17.6%	

Transform the following percentages into decimals, rounding off to 3 decimal places.

	QUESTION	ANSWER
35.	20.85%	
36.	85.6%	
37.	98.88%	

Transform the following numbers into percentages, rounding off to 1 decimal place.

	QUESTION	ANSWER
38.	0.287	
39.	0.4555	
40.	2.4051	

You could come across many types of question involving percentages in a numerical reasoning test. We will go through these in detail in the following sections. Each type of question requires a different computation, and this means that when you are completing the test you must concentrate on reading the question so that you immediately understand which type of calculation is required to solve the question.

QUESTION: What is x% of A?
GENERAL SOLUTION: Divide x by 100, and multiply this by A.
FORMULA: $A \times (x \div 100)$

SAMPLE QUESTION: What is 12% of 50?
SOLUTION: You have to work out 50 × (12 ÷ 100) = 50 × 0.12
= 6, so the answer is 6.

Note that in order to make the calculations required, you had to transform the percentage, 12 per cent, into a decimal, 0.12. Having solved the practice questions, you should be able to make this transformation without using a calculator, which will save you time during the test. Try to solve the following examples as quickly as possible, using a calculator for the computations but not for transforming the percentages into decimals.

Practice questions

	QUESTION	ANSWER
41.	What is 20% of 200?	
42.	What is 15% of 350?	
43.	What is 48% of 500?	

Now that you know how to work through this type of percentage calculation, all you need do is recognize when it is required by a question. Look at the questions below. They all talk about different things, but in essence they require you to find a specific percentage of a given value.

Sample questions

....

QUESTION	ANSWER

44. If there is a 30% discount on a £12 bottle of wine how much money do you save on this purchase?

....

45. If 300 people, of whom 45% were women, attended a conference how many women attended the conference?

....

46. If a 250-hour light bulb worked for only 78% of its 'life' for how many hours did it work?

....

Essentially, what you need to do is practise the computations for the different types of question and learn to recognize each type.

QUESTION: What is x as a percentage of A?
SOLUTION: Divide x by A and transform this into a percentage.
FORMULA: $(x \div A) \times 100\%$

SAMPLE QUESTION: What is 9 as a percentage of 20?
SOLUTION: You have to work out $9 \div 20$. This will give you 0.45, which you have to transform into a percentage, so the answer is 45 per cent.

Now work through the following examples, rounding off your answers to one decimal place.

Practice questions

QUESTION	ANSWER
47. What is 1 as a percentage of 4?	
48. What is 15 as a percentage of 75?	
49. What is 37 as a percentage of 70?	

Sample questions

QUESTION	ANSWER
50. What percentage of the total sales made were due to laptops if total sales were £750,000 and sales due to laptops were £220,000?	
51. What percentage of water consumption was caused by the washing machine if water consumption was 20,000 litres and the washing machine consumed 1,500 litres?	
52. What percentage of the floor is covered by the carpet if the floor is 75 metres^2 and the carpet is 40 metres^2?	

QUESTION: What is A increased by x%?
SOLUTION: Add x to 100. Divide this by 100 and then multiply this by A.
FORMULA: $A \times [(100 + x) \div 100]$

SAMPLE QUESTION: What is 20 increased by 2%?
SOLUTION: You have to work out 20 × [(100 + 2) ÷ 100] = 20 × (102 ÷ 100) = 20 × 1.02, so the answer is 20.4.

TIP: When you have to work out this kind of question, there is a shortcut you can use rather than going through all these calculations. Transform x into decimals and add 1. This has the same value as [(100 + x) ÷ 100]. If you multiply this directly by A you will get your answer. In the example given, transforming 2 per cent into 0.02 and adding 1, will give you 1.02. Now multiply this by 20 and you have your answer. As you can see, this just takes you directly to the final answer, skipping the first two steps and saving time. Try to solve the following examples by using this shortcut.

Practice questions

	QUESTION	ANSWER
53.	What is 2,500 increased by 25%?	
54.	What is 320 increased by 40%?	
55.	What is 500 increased by 125%?	

TIP: Do not get confused when the question is about an increase that is over 100 per cent. For example, if you have to calculate 500 increased by 125 per cent, you have to work out 500 × [(125 + 100) ÷ 100] = 500 × (225 ÷ 100)) = 500 × 2.25. Using the shortcut, this would be 500 × (1.25 + 1) = 500 × 2.25. A common mistake here would be to multiply 500 by just 1.25. This would give you an increase of 0.25 rather than 1.25.

Sample questions

	QUESTION	ANSWER
56.	If the temperature is 15°C and rises by 20%, what will it become?	
57.	If the production of light bulbs increases from 5 million parts by 3% how many parts will be produced?	
58.	What will Mike's salary be if he gets a 15% rise on his current £30,000 a year?	

A more complicated variation on this question is when you are asked about a successive percentage increase. Look, for example, at the following question.

	QUESTION	ANSWER
59.	If a company's profits increase from £800,000 by 10% a year what will they be in three years' time?	

In order to solve this question, you need to calculate the percentage increase successively for each year. So you need to work out:

In 1 year: 800,000 × 1.10 = 880,000
In 2 years: 880,000 × 1.10 = 968,000
In 3 years: 968,000 × 1.10 = 1,064,800

So the answer is £1,064,800. This is not a more difficult question; it just requires you to make the same calculations more than once.

QUESTION: What is A decreased by x%?

SOLUTION: Subtract *x* from 100, divide this value by 100 and multiply by A.

FORMULA: $A \times [(100 - x) \div 100)]$

SAMPLE QUESTION: What is 50 decreased by 8%?

SOLUTION: You have to work out 50 × [(100 − 8) ÷ 100] = 50 × (92 ÷ 100) = 50 × 0.92, so the answer is 46.

TIP: As with the increase in percentages, there is a shortcut for the decrease in percentages. You should again transform *x* per cent into decimals and this time subtract it from 1. Multiply this value by A to get to the answer directly. In the example above, if you transform 8 per cent to 0.08 and subtract this from 1, you will get 0.92. Multiply this by 50 and you are at the final computation that gives you the answer. This method is faster, but it requires you to work out 1− 0.08. This is an example of the simple calculations that were given in the beginning of this section coming in handy.

Practice questions

	QUESTION	ANSWER
60.	What is 100 decreased by 25%?	
61.	What is 250 decreased by 15%?	
62.	What is 2,000,000 decreased by 2.5%?	

Sample questions

QUESTION	ANSWER
63. How many employees will a company have if 20% of its 150 employees are made redundant?	
64. How many words should an essay have if its 4,500 words should be reduced by 15%?	
65. How many cows are healthy if 8% of the 350 cows are sick?	

QUESTION: What is the percentage increase from A to B?
SOLUTION: Divide B by A, and subtract 1 from the value you obtain. Then transform this into a percentage.
FORMULA: $[(B \div A) - 1] \times 100\%$

SAMPLE QUESTION: What is the percentage increase from 20 to 30?
SOLUTION: You have to work out $(30 \div 20) - 1 = 1.5 - 1 = 0.5$. Transform this back to a percentage, so the answer is 50%.

Note that this requires the opposite calculation from the question asking 'What is 20 increased by 50 per cent?' Remember that for that question, the solution required you to add 0.5 to 1 (this was explained in the tip), which is 1.5, and to multiply this by 20, yielding 30.

TIP: Do not get confused when the increase is over 100 per cent. For example, if you have to calculate the percentage increase from 10 to 30, you have to work out $(30 \div 10) - 1 = 3 - 1 = 2$. Transform this to a percentage, so the answer is 200 per cent. A common mistake here would be to calculate $30 \div 10$, which is 3, and then forget to subtract 1 from this. This would give the answer that the increase was 300%. However, 10 increased by 300 per cent is actually 40, not 30.

Practice questions

....

QUESTION	ANSWER

66. What is the percentage increase from 70 to 75?

....

67. What is the percentage increase from 250 to 550?

....

68. What is the percentage increase from 150 to 175?

....

Sample questions

....

QUESTION	ANSWER

69. What is the percentage increase in John's height if he grows from 1.65 metres to 1.75 metres?

....

70. What is the percentage increase of the time you have to complete a 20-minute test if you are allowed 25 minutes to complete it?

....

71. What is the percentage increase of your monthly savings if they go from £250 to £310?

....

QUESTION: What is the percentage decrease from B to A?

SOLUTION: Subtract A from B, and divide this by B. Transform this into a percentage.

FORMULA: $[(B - A) \div B] \times 100\%$

SAMPLE QUESTION: What is the percentage decrease from 200 to 150?

SOLUTION: You have to work out $[(200 - 150) \div 200] = 50 \div 200 = 0.25$. Transform this back into a percentage, so the answer is 25%.

TIP: When you are performing this type of calculation try to subtract A from B in your head in order to save time.

Practice questions

QUESTION	ANSWER
72. What is the percentage decrease from 8 to 5?	
73. What is the percentage decrease from 125 to 75?	
74. What is the percentage decrease from 175 to 100?	

Sample questions

....

QUESTION	ANSWER

75. What is the percentage decrease of someone's weight if they go from 85 kilograms to 82 kilograms?

....

76. What is the percentage decrease in the time you work if you go from a 37.5 hours a week job to a 22.5 hours a week job?

....

77. What is the percentage decrease of a 20,000 metre^2 forest if 17,500 metre^2 of the forest survives a fire?

....

Ratios

Ratios are used to make comparisons between two things. The most common way of presenting ratios is by writing 'the ratio of A to B' or by writing A:B. Note that if the ratio of A to B is 3:1, this simply means that A is 3 times greater than B. As with percentages, there are various types of questions that can involve ratios. These are detailed in the pages that follow.

QUESTION: What is the ratio of A to B, if A = a and B = b?
SOLUTION: Divide a by b. This quotient to 1 is the ratio of a to b.
FORMULA: $a \div b : 1$

> **SAMPLE QUESTION:** What is the ratio of A to B, if A = 20 and
>   B = 25?
> **SOLUTION:** The ratio of A to B is 20 ÷ 25 : 1 = 0.8:1.

Practice questions

Solve the following examples, rounding off your answers where necessary
to 2 decimal places.

	QUESTION	ANSWER
78.	What is the ratio of A:B, if A = 600 and B = 150?	
79.	What is the ratio of A:B, if A = 0.2 and B = 0.8?	
80.	What is the ratio of A:B, if A = 46 and B = 55.5?	

Sample questions

	QUESTION	ANSWER
81.	What is the ratio of males to females in a group if there are 66 males and 60 females in the group?	
82.	What is the ratio of examples to practice questions if there are 90 examples and 480 practice questions?	
83.	What is the ratio of John's to Harry's racing medals if John has 15 medals and Harry has 6?	

Another type of question involving ratios is when you are given the ratio of two groups and the size of one of the two groups and are asked to calculate the size of the second group.

QUESTION: If the ratio of A to B is x:y, and B = b, what is the size of A?
SOLUTION: Divide x by y, and multiply this quotient by b.
FORMULA: $b \times (x \div y)$

SAMPLE QUESTION: If the ratio of laptops to desktops is 3:2, and there are 50 desktops, how many laptops are there?
SOLUTION: You have to work out $50 \times (3 \div 2) = 50 \times 1.5 = 75$. Similarly, you may be given the value of A and asked to work out the value of B.

QUESTION: If the ratio of A to B is x:y, and A = a, what is the size of B?
SOLUTION: Divide y by x and multiply this quotient by a.
FORMULA: $a \times (y \div x)$

SAMPLE QUESTION: If the ratio of laptops to desktops is 4:1 and there are 60 laptops, how many desktops are there?
SOLUTION: You have to work out $60 \times (1 \div 4) = 60 \times 0.25 = 15$.

Practice questions

	QUESTION	ANSWER
84.	If the ratio of A to B is 4:1, and B = 10, what is the size of A?	
85.	If the ratio of A to B is 4:5, and B = 90, what is the size of A?	
86.	If the ratio of A to B is 3:4, and A is 60.5, what is the size of B?	

Sample questions

	QUESTION	ANSWER
87.	If the ratio of fish to cats in a pet shop is 6:1 and there are 24 fish, how many cats are there?	
88.	If the ratio of non-smoking to smoking tables in a restaurant is 7:2 and there are 6 smoking tables, how many non-smoking tables are there?	
89.	If the ratio of restaurants to bars in a town is 1.5:1 and there are 20 bars, how many restaurants are there?	

Another type of question on ratios is when you are given the total number of a group and the ratio of its subgroups and are asked to find the size of the subgroups.

QUESTION: If A consists of B and C, and the ratio of B to C is x:y, what is the size of B?

SOLUTION: Divide x by the sum of x and y, and multiply this quotient by A.

FORMULA: $A \times [x \div (x + y)]$

SAMPLE QUESTION: If there are 90 students in a lecture theatre, with a male to female ratio of 2:1, how many males are in the lecture theatre?

SOLUTION: You have to work out $90 \times [2 \div (2+1)] = 90 \times 2 \div 3 = 60$. Similarly, you could be given the value of B and asked for the value of C. The question then would be as follows.

QUESTION: If A consists of B and C and the ratio of B to C is x:y, what is the size of C?

SOLUTION: Divide y by the sum of x and y and multiply this quotient by A.

FORMULA: $A \times [y \div (x + y)]$

SAMPLE QUESTION: If there are 80 employees in a company, with a male to female ratio of 3:1, how many females work in the company?

SOLUTION: You have to work out $80 \times [1 \div (3+1)] = 80 \times 1 \div 4 = 20$.

Practice questions

Work out the following examples, for a total (A) of 100, rounding off your answers to 2 decimal places.

QUESTION	ANSWER
90. What is the size of B, if the ratio of B to C is 1:4?	
91. What is the size of C, if the ratio of B to C is 1:3?	
92. What is the size of B, if the ratio of B to C is 3:2?	

Sample questions

Work out the following questions, given that the total population of Malta is 400,000. Round off your answers to whole numbers.

QUESTION	ANSWER
93. How many women are there in Malta if the male to female ratio is 0.99:1?	
94. How many people are over 14 in Malta if the ratio of people aged 14 or less to people aged over 14 is 1:5.4?	
95. How many people are under 60 in Malta if the ratio of people aged less than 60 to people aged 60 or more is 7:1?	

Ways of presenting numerical data

Numerical reasoning questions can include the numerical data within the questions themselves or the data can be presented separately – in a table, graph, bar chart, pie chart and so on. So that you can compare the different ways of presenting information, the same data are presented below in different formats.

Data presented in a table

FIGURE 1: **Earthquakes in the US (by magnitude)**

	2001	2002	2003	2004	2005
0.1–3.9	800	1500	1300	1400	1500
4.0–4.9	1000	1700	1000	1900	1800
5.0–9.9	300	600	600	300	400
Total	2100	3800	2900	3600	3700

Data presented in a bar chart

FIGURE 2: **Earthquakes in the US (by magnitude)**

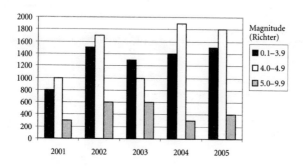

Below is another way of presenting the same data in a different type of bar chart.

FIGURE 3: Earthquakes in the US (by magnitude)

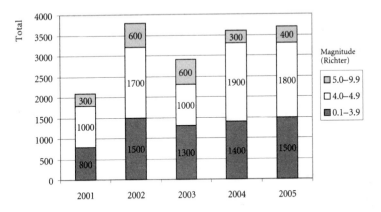

Data presented in a graph

FIGURE 4: Earthquakes in the US (by magnitude)

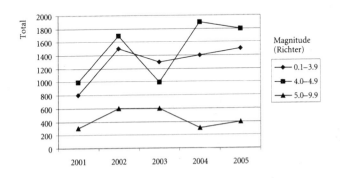

Data presented in pie charts

FIGURE 5: **Earthquakes in the US (by magnitude for 2001 and 2002)**

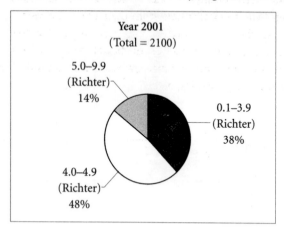

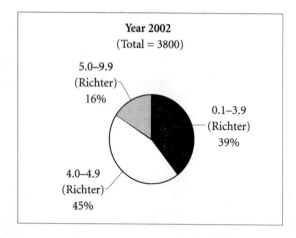

These are a few ways in which data can be presented, and they are the most usual ways in which data are presented in numerical reasoning tests. What type of questions could you come across in a test that presents the numerical information in the above formats?

Questions related to tables, graphs and so on could be simple questions that look at whether you are able to extract the relevant data from the table and perform simple calculations. Other questions however, will require you to extract data from the table and perform calculations such as those presented in the section on Further Numerical Calculations (see pages 32–52). In the following sections you will be presented with various practice questions that are linked to the different formats of presenting data.

Questions based on tables

Take as an example Figure 1 and answer the practice questions, rounding off to the nearest whole number.

FIGURE 1: **Earthquakes in the US (by magnitude)**

	2001	2002	2003	2004	2005
0.1–3.9	800	1500	1300	1400	1500
4.0–4.9	1000	1700	1000	1900	1800
5.0–9.9	300	600	600	300	400
Total	2100	3800	2900	3600	3700

Practice questions

	QUESTION	ANSWER
96.	How many more 4.0–4.9 earthquakes were there in 2004 than in 2003?	
97.	On average, how many 5.0–9.9 earthquakes were there between 2001 and 2005?	
98.	By what percentage did the total number of earthquakes increase between 2003 and 2004?	
99.	What percentage of the total earthquakes in 2005 were 0.1–3.9 earthquakes?	
100.	What was the ratio of 0.1–3.9 to 4.0–4.9 earthquakes in 2003?	

It is important to pay attention to detail. The questions above were all straightforward, but make sure that you do not make assumptions that are not true. Look, for example, at the following questions.

QUESTION	ANSWER

101. How many more earthquakes were there in 2005 than in 2003?

Because you are in a hurry you might assume that the question was asking about an increase between two consecutive years. This is not always the case.

QUESTION	ANSWER

102. On average, how many 0.1–3.9 earthquakes were there a year between 2002 and 2005?

Again, you might assume that you are being asked to calculate the average of all the values presented to you, but this is not always the case. Make sure that you pay attention to detail and look at the correct data.

Numerical reasoning tests that include data presented to you in a graph, chart or similar format will typically give you a multiple choice of answers from which you have to choose the correct one. The practice questions on the following pages will, therefore, be in this format so that you can familiarize yourself with the format that you are most likely to face.

FIGURE 6: Car and mobile phone ownership in Finland

| House type | 1996 | | | 1999 | | |
	No. of houses	% of houses owning a car	% of houses owning a mobile phone	No. of houses	% of houses owning a car	% of houses owning a mobile phone
1-person	860,000	40	35	950,000	52	66
2-person	680,000	75	35	700,000	85	80
3-person	320,000	92	54	300,000	92	90
4-person	290,000	95	64	280,000	98	97
5-person	60,000	95	51	60,000	100	95
All	2,230,000	68	42	2,350,000	74	78

Practice questions

....

QUESTION   ANSWER

103. How many 5-person households owned a mobile
phone in 1996 in Finland?

   a. 30,600

   b. 55,000

   c. 56,000

   d. 57,000

   e. 60,000

....

QUESTION   ANSWER

104. By approximately what percentage did the number
of 4-person households decrease between 1996
and 1999 in Finland?

    a. 3.3%
    b. 3.5%
    c. 3.7%
    d. 3.9%
    e. 4.1%

QUESTION   ANSWER

105. How many people were living in a 2- or a 3-person
household in 1999 in Finland, in thousands?

    a. 1,000
    b. 2,220
    c. 2,300
    d. 2,320
    e. 2,350

QUESTION   ANSWER

106. In 1996 what was the radio of 2-person
households to 3-person households in Finland?

    a. 2:1
    b. 2.25:1
    c. 2.5:1
    d. 2.75:1
    e. 3:1

QUESTION	ANSWER

107. If the number of 1-person households owning a car increased by 10% each year from 1999, how many 1-person households owned a car in 2001?

  a. 543,400
  b. 597,740
  c. 642,200
  d. 675,514
  e. 1,264,450

'Cannot Say' option

The multiple-choice answers in numerical reasoning tests occasionally include a 'Cannot Say' option, and you should choose this option if the information provided in the graph is not sufficient for you to calculate the answer. These questions are typically based on extrapolating in some sense. This means that you could perform calculations from the information given in order to extrapolate the answer, but your answer will be an estimate and not definitely the correct answer. Look, for example, at the questions below, which are linked to the data presented in Figure 6 (see page 58).

QUESTION	ANSWER

108. How many 3-person households were there in Finland in 1998?

  a. 280,000
  b. 285,000
  c. 290,000
  d. 310,000
  e. Cannot Say

QUESTION	ANSWER

109. What percentage of houses owned a car and a mobile phone in 1999?

a. 6%
b. 74%
c. 76%
d. 78%
e. Cannot Say

QUESTION	ANSWER

110. What was the percentage increase of 3-person houses owning a car between 1996 and 1998?

a. 0%
b. 10%
c. 36%
d. 92%
e. Cannot Say

The correct answers to questions 108–110 are 'Cannot Say'. Even though you could guess at the answer in each case, there is no information in the data indicating that your assumption is correct. So the advice is, when there is a 'Cannot Say' option among the answers, make sure that you do not make any assumptions in order to derive an answer. If you need to make an assumption in order to calculate an answer, the correct answer is actually 'Cannot Say'.

Questions based on bar charts

FIGURE 7: Toaster Defects in Yorkshire, Lancashire and Hampshire

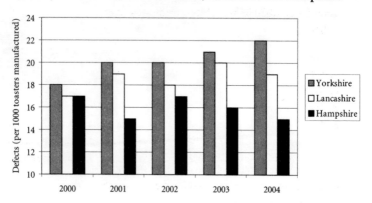

Practice questions

....

QUESTION   ANSWER

111. In which year was the total number of defects per
1,000 toasters the greatest?

    a. 2000   **b.** 2001   **c.** 2002
    d. 2003   **e.** 2004

....

QUESTION   ANSWER

112. What was the overall percentage increase in the
number of defects per 1,000 toasters in Yorkshire,
across the five years?

    a. 21.11%   **b.** 22.22%   **c.** 23.33%
    d. 24.44%   **e.** 25.55%

....

QUESTION   ANSWER

113. What was the ratio of the number of toaster defects per 1,000 in Yorkshire to Hampshire in 2001?

    a. 1:3
    b. 3:4
    c. 4:3
    d. 3:2
    e. 3:1

QUESTION   ANSWER

114. Over the five years, what was the average annual number of defects per 1,000 toasters in Hampshire?

    a. 15
    b. 16
    c. 17
    d. 18
    e. Cannot Say

QUESTION   ANSWER

115. If about 2.3 million toasters were manufactured in the Lancashire factory in 2004, how many toasters had defects?

    a. 43,500
    b. 43,600
    c. 43,700
    d. 43,800
    e. 43,900

FIGURE 8: Colour of manufactured cars

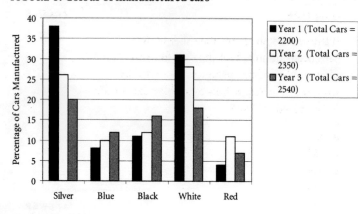

Practice questions

QUESTION   ANSWER

116. How many more silver cars than red cars were
there in Year 1?

    a. 740
    b. 742
    c. 744
    d. 746
    e. 748

QUESTION   ANSWER

117. Over the three years about how many white cars
were produced?

    a. 1,775
    b. 1,786
    c. 1,797
    d. 1,808
    e. 1,819

QUESTION   ANSWER

118. If the trend in the percentage of blue cars
produced continued for the next five years and the
total number of cars produced increased by 15%
from Year 3 to Year 6, how many blue cars would
be produced in Year 6?

a. 526
b. 530
c. 534
d. 538
e. 542

QUESTION   ANSWER

119. In Year 2, if 20% of cars painted with other colours
were green, how many green cars were produced?

a. 60
b. 61
c. 62
d. 63
e. 64

QUESTION   ANSWER

120. If, from Year 3 to Year 4, there was the same
percentage increase in total car production as
there was from Year 2 to Year 3, yet the percentage
of black cars remained constant, how many black
cars were produced in Year 4?

a. 419
b. 429
c. 439
d. 449
e. 459

Question based on graphs

Figure 9: Market share

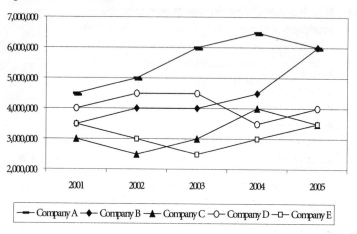

Practice questions

....

QUESTION   ANSWER

121. What was average revenue earned by the five
companies in 2003?

    a. £ 4.0 million   **b.** £ 4.5 million
    c. £ 5.5 million   **d.** £ 18.0 million
    e. £ 20.0 million

....

QUESTION   ANSWER

122. In 2004 Company B had 15% of the total market.
What was the total market worth?

    a. £ 4.5 million   **b.** £ 17.5 million
    c. £ 25.5 million   **d.** £ 30.0 million
    e. £ 67.5 million

....

QUESTION   ANSWER

123. Which company had the lowest average revenue over the five years?

   a. Company A
   b. Company B
   c. Company C
   d. Company D
   e. Company E

QUESTION   ANSWER

124. Between 2002 and 2005 which company proportionately increased its revenue the most?

   a. Company A
   b. Company B
   c. Company C
   d. Company D
   e. Company E

QUESTION   ANSWER

125. If the percentage increase in Company E's revenue between 2004 and 2005 is the same in the following year, what will Company E's revenue be in 2006?

   a. £ 3.60 million
   b. £ 3.74 million
   c. £ 3.89 million
   d. £ 4.08 million
   e. £ 4.57 million

Questions based on pie charts

FIGURE 10: Population composition for east and west regions

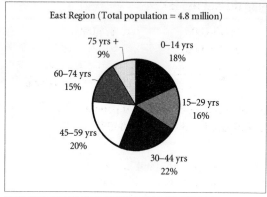

East Region (Total population = 4.8 million)

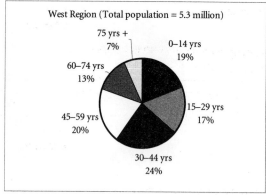

West Region (Total population = 5.3 million)

Practice questions

....

QUESTION   ANSWER

126. How many 15- to 29-year-olds live in the west
region?

a. 749,000   b. 791,000   c. 849,000
d. 901,000   e. 959,000

....

QUESTION | ANSWER

127. How many more 30- to 44-year-olds live in the west region than in the east region?

    a. 116,000   **b.** 136,000   **c.** 176,000
    d. 196,000   **e.** 216,000

QUESTION | ANSWER

128. In the east region what is the proportion of people aged 60 or older compared to those aged 30–59 years?

    a. 54.1%   **b.** 57.1%   **c.** 60.1%
    d. 63.1%   **e.** 67.1%

QUESTION | ANSWER

129. How many more people aged under 30 live in the west region than in the east region?

    a. 256,000   **b.** 266,000   **c.** 276,000
    d. 286,000   **e.** 296,000

QUESTION | ANSWER

130. If the number of 60- to 74-year-olds were to increase by 5% in the next ten years, how many more 60- to 74-year-olds would there be in both regions?

    a. 70,450   **b.** 73,650   **c.** 75,200
    d. 77,250   **e.** 79,400

Other numerical reasoning questions

Number sequences

A different type of question that you may find in a numerical reasoning test are questions based on number sequences. A sequence is essentially a string of values that have a pattern from one number to the next. Questions on sequences will typically give you several numbers in a row and ask you to find either the missing number or the next number in the sequence.

The more you practise with solving questions on sequences, the easier they will become. This is because sequences often follow specific patterns, and if you have already found a pattern once, it will be easier to observe it again with different numbers.

Practice questions

Find the number that should replace '?' in the following sequences.

QUESTION	ANSWER
131. 1, 4, ?, 16, 25, 36 . . .	

    a. 6
    b. 8
    c. 9
    d. 12
    e. 15

QUESTION	ANSWER
132. 1, 2, 4, 7, 11, ? . . .	

    a. 12
    b. 14
    c. 15
    d. 16
    e. 17

QUESTION   ANSWER

133. 6, 12, 24, ?, 96, 192 . . .

   a. 36
   b. 38
   c. 42
   d. 48
   e. 66

QUESTION   ANSWER

134. 3, 4, 2, 5, 1, 6, ? . . .

   a. 0
   b. 1
   c. 2
   d. 3
   e. 4

QUESTION   ANSWER

135. 1, 3, 7, ?, 31, 63 . . .

   a. 13
   b. 15
   c. 17
   d. 18
   e. 23

QUESTION   ANSWER

136. 2, 5, 8, 11, 14, 17, ?, 23, 26 . . .

   a. 18
   b. 19
   c. 20
   d. 21
   e. 22

QUESTION

ANSWER

137. 1, 2, 5, 10, 17, 26, ? ...

   a. 33
   b. 34
   c. 35
   d. 36
   e. 37

QUESTION

ANSWER

138. 50, 49, ?, 41, 34, 25 ...

   a. 43
   b. 44
   c. 45
   d. 46
   e. 47

QUESTION

ANSWER

139. 1, 2, 4, 7, 11, 16, 22, ?, 37

   a. 27
   b. 28
   c. 29
   d. 30
   e. 31

QUESTION

ANSWER

140. 27, 23, 19, ?, 11, 7, 3 ...

   a. 13
   b. 15
   c. 16
   d. 17
   e. 18

QUESTION	ANSWER

141. 1, 4, 9, 16, ?, 36, 49, 64 . . .

    a. 18
    b. 20
    c. 24
    d. 25
    e. 30

QUESTION	ANSWER

142. 1, 2, 4, 5, 10, 11, 22, 23, 46, 47, ? . . .

    a. 50
    b. 60
    c. 70
    d. 84
    e. 94

QUESTION	ANSWER

143. 1, 3, ?, 4, 3, 5, 4, 6, 5, 7 . . .

    a. 1
    b. 2
    c. 3
    d. 4
    e. 5

QUESTION	ANSWER

144. 12, 23, 34, 45, 56, ?, 78, 89 . . .

    a. 60
    b. 64
    c. 67
    d. 69
    e. 73

QUESTION   ANSWER

145.   5, 10, 17, 20, 29, 30, 41, 40, ?, 50, 65

    a. 43
    b. 45
    c. 49
    d. 53
    e. 57

QUESTION   ANSWER

146.   10, 8, 9, 6, 8, 4, 7, 2, 6, ? . . .

    a. 0
    b. 1
    c. 2
    d. 4
    e. 5

QUESTION   ANSWER

147.   2, 5, 10, 17, 26, ?, 50, 65 . . .

    a. 37
    b. 38
    c. 39
    d. 40
    e. 47

QUESTION   ANSWER

148.   10.5, 11.8, 13.1, 14.4, 15.7, ?, 18.3 . . .

    a. 15.9
    b. 16.3
    c. 16.5
    d. 16.7
    e. 17.0

QUESTION	ANSWER

149. 1, 3, 4, 7, 11, 18, 29, ?, 76, 123 . . .

    a. 37
    b. 43
    c. 47
    d. 52
    e. 56

QUESTION	ANSWER

150. 1, 1, -2, -6, 24, ?, -720 . . .

    a. -120
    b. -96
    c. 36
    d. 96
    e. 120

Other non-graphical questions

Practice questions

QUESTION	ANSWER

151. If one typist can type three pages in 2 minutes, how many minutes would it take three typists to type 12 pages?

    a. 4
    b. 5
    c. 6
    d. 7
    e. 8

QUESTION   ANSWER

152. A car travels at a constant 30 mph for half an hour,
after which the car's speed averages 60 mph for the
next half-hour. How far has the car travelled?

    a. 30 miles
    b. 37.5 miles
    c. 40 miles
    d. 45 miles
    e. 47.5 miles

QUESTION   ANSWER

153. In 90 minutes' time, it will be half as close to
midnight as it is now. What time is it now?

    a. 19:30
    b. 20:00
    c. 20:30
    d. 21:00
    e. 22:00

QUESTION   ANSWER

154. A retailer buys 30 jackets at £52.49 each and twice
as many trousers at £45.99 each. How much
remains from a budget of £5,000?

    a. £490.90
    b. £665.90
    c. £908.80
    d. £1,585.90
    e. £2,045.60

QUESTION

ANSWER

155. A company has profits of £45,000, of which 20% will be paid as tax. The remaining profit will be split among three owners, of which one owns as much as the other two together. How much will the majority owner receive?

a. £9,000
b. £12,000
c. £15,000
d. £18,000
e. £22,500

QUESTION

ANSWER

156. If a company makes 3,500 pens in a five-day working week, in which a day has 7 working hours, how many pens are made in one hour?

a. 35
b. 70
c. 100
d. 350
e. 700

QUESTION

ANSWER

157. A page of stickers measures 30 cm by 40 cm. If each sticker is 3 cm by 5 cm, what is the maximum number of stickers that will fit on the page with no overlap?

a. 20
b. 40
c. 60
d. 80
e. 100

QUESTION   ANSWER

158. Green pens cost one and a half times as much as
red pens, which cost twice as much as blue pens. If
a blue pen costs 20p, how many green pens can
you get for £5.40?

    a. 5
    b. 6
    c. 7
    d. 8
    e. 9

QUESTION   ANSWER

159. Five men each order a drink for £2.89 and a bag of
crisps for 65p. If one man paid for all the crisps
and drinks with a £20 note how much change
would he get?

    a. £2.30
    b. £5.84
    c. £9.45
    d. £14.16
    e. £17.70

QUESTION   ANSWER

160. In a factory that manufactures kettles 10% of all
those made are green and 20% are red. If 500
kettles are made in a week how many red and
green kettles will have been made in one year?

    a. 100
    b. 150
    c. 780
    d. 5,200
    e. 7,800

QUESTION	ANSWER

161. A car took 24 minutes to finish a journey. If it travelled at an average speed of 45 km an hour, how far did it travel?

    a. 12 km
    b. 18 km
    c. 24 km
    d. 27 km
    e. 32 km

QUESTION	ANSWER

162. How many apples can you buy with £1.60 if an apple costs 26p?

    a. 4
    b. 5
    c. 6
    d. 7
    e. 8

QUESTION	ANSWER

163. A printer prints 40 pages in a minute. How long will it take to print 35 copies of a document 120 pages long?

    a. 42 mins
    b. 1 hr 5 mins
    c. 1 hr 25 mins
    d. 1 hr 45 mins
    e. 2 hrs 15 mins

QUESTION   ANSWER

164. How many 37.5 cl cups of orange juice can be
filled from a 300 cl bottle?

    a. 6
    b. 7
    c. 8
    d. 16
    e. 80

QUESTION   ANSWER

165. For every four cans of cola bought, you receive
two cans extra free. If each can costs 50p each how
much would you pay for 24 cans?

    a. £2
    b. £4
    c. £6
    d. £8
    e. £10

4 Verbal reasoning tests

Verbal reasoning tests assess your ability to reason with information that is presented to you in a verbal format. There are several types of verbal reasoning test, including tests of spelling, of word comprehension and of word analogies, which are discussed in the following sections. However, the type of verbal reasoning test you are most likely to face within a recruitment procedure is a test of text comprehension.

Tests of comprehension will typically include a number of short passages of text followed by a number of statements. Candidates are asked to indicate whether the statements are true, false or 'Cannot Say' based on the information in the text. A variation of this is when you are presented with a number of statements and have to decide which is most true, again based on the information in the text. Tests of text comprehension are discussed in the last two sections of this chapter.

Spelling tests

Spelling tests simply assess your ability to spell correctly. They can take a number of forms. For example, you could be presented with a number of different spellings of the same word and have to choose the correct one. Alternatively, you could be presented with sentences with missing words and have to choose the word with the correct spelling.

You could argue that practising spelling tests will not really help, because your performance will depend on whether you know the words that are in the actual test. It is true that if you come across words that you have not previously encountered, practising will not help much, but with practice you will unconsciously observe the rules that will help you in spelling 'new' words. In addition, practice will increase the chances that you will already have seen a word that is in the test.

Spelling test 1

Practice questions

Of the words presented below, choose the one that is spelled correctly.

166.	**a.** accomodate	**b.** acommodate	**c.** accommodate
167.	**a.** occasionally	**b.** occasionaly	**c.** occassionally
168.	**a.** irresistable	**b.** irresistible	**c.** iresistible
169.	**a.** succeful	**b.** successfull	**c.** successful
170.	**a.** commitment	**b.** committment	**c.** comitment
171.	**a.** irreversable	**b.** irreversible	**c.** ireversable
172.	**a.** ficticious	**b.** fictiscious	**c.** fictitious
173.	**a.** enpowerment	**b.** empowernment	**c.** empowerment
174.	**a.** liase	**b.** liaise	**c.** lieise
175.	**a.** comfortable	**b.** confortable	**c.** comfortible
176.	**a.** usefull	**b.** usefful	**c.** useful
177.	**a.** carelesness	**b.** carelessness	**c.** carelessnes
178.	**a.** definetely	**b.** definately	**c.** definitely

179.	a. separately	b. separetly	c. saparetely
180.	a. couragously	b. couragiously	c. courageously
181.	a. idiosincracy	b. idiosyncrasy	c. idiosincrasy
182.	a. consistently	b. consistantly	c. consistantley
183.	a. correspondant	b. correspondent	c. corespondent

Spelling test 2

Practice questions

Choose the word that is missing from the following sentences.

QUESTION   ANSWER

184. Dr Hopkins explained the most important
_____ of relativity.

a. principle
b. principal
c. prenciple

QUESTION   ANSWER

185. I would be _____ if you could help me with
this assignment.

a. greatful
b. grateful
c. gratefull

QUESTION	ANSWER

186. Samantha was _____ proud of her dissertation.

   a. especialy
   b. especially
   c. espescially

QUESTION	ANSWER

187. Last weekend's football game provided the largest _____ in the club's history.

   a. receipts
   b. reciepts
   c. receits

QUESTION	ANSWER

188. The latest _____ of the new drugs has produced encouraging results.

   a. trialling
   b. trialing
   c. tryling

QUESTION	ANSWER

189. The answer he gave was _____ to the question they asked him.

   a. irrelevant
   b. irellevant
   c. irelevant

QUESTION	ANSWER

190. Microscopes help with the viewing of _____ objects.

    a. minniscule
    b. minuscule
    c. minnuscule

QUESTION	ANSWER

191. At night _____ can be scary places.

    a. cemetaries
    b. cemmeteries
    c. cemeteries

QUESTION	ANSWER

192. A _____ is a feature of many democracies.

    a. parliament
    b. parliamment
    c. parlamment

QUESTION	ANSWER

193. _____ can be used to prune house plants.

    a. scisors
    b. sissors
    c. scissors

QUESTION	ANSWER

194. _____ is nine-tenths of the law.

   a. possession
   b. possesion
   c. posession

QUESTION	ANSWER

195. The pink dress is _____.

   a. preferrable
   b. preferable
   c. prefferable

QUESTION	ANSWER

196. Mr Smith's behaviour at the party was highly
_____.

   a. embarrasing
   b. embarassing
   c. embarrassing

QUESTION	ANSWER

197. It has been a _____ to have worked with
you.

   a. privilege
   b. privilage
   c. privillege

QUESTION	ANSWER

198. A _____ contains no air.

    a. vaccum
    b. vacuum
    c. vacume

QUESTION	ANSWER

199. Art deco lamps are becoming far more

    _____.

    a. collectable
    b. colectable
    c. colectible

QUESTION	ANSWER

200. The broken pipes will be repaired by the
_____ department.

    a. maintainance
    b. maintenence
    c. maintenance

QUESTION	ANSWER

201. The costing for this project is _____.

    a. ridiculus
    b. ridiculous
    c. rediculous

QUESTION	ANSWER

202. It is only _____ that I check my spellings.

    a. occasionally
    b. ocassionally
    c. occassionaly

QUESTION	ANSWER

203. Some school children can be very _____.

    a. mischivous
    b. mischeivous
    c. mischievous

Practice websites

If you feel you want to practise with spelling tests, there are a few websites from which you can access practice tests for free:

http://www.sentex.net/~mmcadams/spelling.html
http://www.buzzin.net/english/spel-x.htm
http://homepage.ntlworld.com/vivian.c/TestsFrame.htm

Word comprehension

Word comprehension tests assess your understanding of the meaning of words. They typically consist of sentences with missing words and require you to choose the word that completes the sentence correctly.

As with spelling tests, the effect of practice will enhance your performance to only a limited extent. However, even if the effect is small, it is always an advantage to practise! This will not only increase the chance that you will have encountered a word that is in the actual test, but it will also help you familiarize yourself with the test format, which will lower your anxiety during the test.

Practice questions

For the sentences presented below, choose the word that is missing.

QUESTION   **ANSWER**

204. Dr Brown was greatly concerned when hearing of the illness with which his patient was _____.

    a. afflicted
    b. affected
    c. affronted

QUESTION   **ANSWER**

205. The choices facing him had placed John in a

_____.

    a. paradox
    b. dilemma
    c. rationalization

QUESTION   ANSWER

206. The maintenance of lifejackets is critical to
_____ the risk of drowning should the boat
capsize.

a. precluding
b. obliterating
c. eradicating

QUESTION   ANSWER

207. Witnesses were _____ in coming forward to
provide statements.

a. repressed
b. subdued
c. reticent

QUESTION   ANSWER

208. Most academics were _____ at the latest
genetic research findings released today.

a. incredulous
b. incredible
c. inductive

QUESTION   ANSWER

209. The beekeeping society meets on _____
Mondays and Wednesdays every other week.

a. alternative
b. alternate
c. alterative

QUESTION   ANSWER

210. The classification of animals involves sorting
species into _____ categories.

    a. continuous
    b. overlapping
    c. discrete

QUESTION   ANSWER

211. The Natqua tribe was known to be _____,
being indifferent to what was right or wrong.

    a. amoral
    b. dissipated
    c. unmoral

QUESTION   ANSWER

212. Detectives are able to solve crimes by observing
and making _____.

    a. implications
    b. inferences
    c. replications

QUESTION   ANSWER

213. The politician's _____ made it difficult to
determine a clear answer to the question.

    a. unambiguity
    b. exaggeration
    c. prevarication

QUESTION	ANSWER

214. The findings of the analysis were highly
_____ compared to the results usually
expected from this experiment.

a. aberrant
b. authentic
c. abhorrent

QUESTION	ANSWER

215. There was a long-stop at the second base camp so
that the climbers could ensure _____ of
their supplies.

a. repletion
b. fulfilment
c. dilation

QUESTION	ANSWER

216. He _____ at the locked door in order to
escape.

a. reclined
b. reposed
c. scrabbled

QUESTION	ANSWER

217. The philosopher's new thoughts were considered
so _____ that few understood them.

a. proficient
b. profound
c. abundant

QUESTION   **ANSWER**

218. The findings of the appeal panel _____
Mr Smith after he was falsely criticized.

    a. exaggerated
    b. exonerated
    c. elevated

QUESTION   **ANSWER**

219. Alkali is an agent that is able to _____ acid
spills effectively.

    a. neutralize
    b. energize
    c. evaporate

QUESTION   **ANSWER**

220. Some parents spend too much time _____
their children when they are naughty.

    a. relegating
    b. abrogating
    c. berating

QUESTION   **ANSWER**

221. The car could not been seen as it drove over a
stream and passed through a _____.

    a. coupe
    b. copse
    c. crevice

QUESTION   ANSWER

222. The speech _____ Brown's views on
economic policy, adding more tension to the
debate.

    a. designated
    b. enveloped
    c. deprecated

QUESTION   ANSWER

223. Although there are many different forms of jazz,
Parker's innovative style could not be described as

    _____.

    a. conformist
    b. religious
    c. dissident

Practice websites

If you feel you want to practise more with word comprehension tests,
there are a few websites from which you can access practice tests for free:

http://www.rhlschool.com/read9n2.htm
http://www.vocabtest.com/hs/senior.htm

Word analogies

Word analogy tests assess your understanding of the relationship between two words. Even though your ability in these sorts of tests will be closely related to your general vocabulary, this is not what word analogy tests are intended to measure, and so the words presented are typically easier than those presented in word comprehension tests.

Word analogy tests typically give you two words that have a particular relationship to each other. You are then presented with a third word and several options. What you have to do is choose the fourth word of the options given, so that the relationship between the third and the fourth words is similar (analogous) to the relationship between the first pair.

Word analogies 1

For the sentences below, circle the word that completes the sentence, so that the analogy is true.

QUESTION	ANSWER

224. Bull is to cow, as stallion is to . . .

    a. mare
    b. mule
    c. horse
    d. calf
    e. gelding

In order to solve this type of question you have to figure out the relationship between the first two words. In the example above the first two words are both animals of the same species, with the second word being the female (cow) and the first word being the male (bull). Therefore the fourth word should be the female of the stallion, which is a mare. So the correct answer is option a.

Practice questions

225. Foot is to shoe as hand is to . . .

   a. finger
   b. glove
   c. arm
   d. hold
   e. wrist

226. Six is to hexagon as five is to . . .

   a. trapezium
   b. parallelogram
   c. pentagon
   d. heptagon
   e. polygon

227. Banana is to yellow as apple is to . . .

   a. orange
   b. blue
   c. black
   d. green
   e. peach

| QUESTION | ANSWER |

228. Pen is to write as scissors are to . . .

    a. paper
    b. cut
    c. sharp
    d. metal
    e. handle

| QUESTION | ANSWER |

229. Greengrocer is to vegetables as butcher is to . . .

    a. meat
    b. fruit
    c. bread
    d. tools
    e. sausages

| QUESTION | ANSWER |

230. Cow is to bovine as sheep is to . . .

    a. covine
    b. ovine
    c. shovine
    d. blovine
    e. lovine

231. Badger is to sett as rabbit is to . . .

    a. den
    b. drey
    c. holt
    d. nest
    e. warren

232. Night is to nocturnal as day is to . . .

    a. light
    b. diurnal
    c. sun
    d. dawn
    e. afternoon

233. Spider is to eight as insect is to . . .

    a. two
    b. four
    c. six
    d. ten
    e. twelve

QUESTION	ANSWER

234. Top is to bottom as left is to . . .

    a. opposite
    b. besides
    c. leave
    d. taken
    e. remain

QUESTION	ANSWER

235. On is to off as fast is to . . .

    a. quick
    b. rapid
    c. sprint
    d. run
    e. eat

QUESTION	ANSWER

236. Rose is to bush as leaf is to . . .

    a. ground
    b. book
    c. page
    d. writing
    e. green

QUESTION   ANSWER

237. Measurement is to length as medium is to . . .

    a. middle
    b. television
    c. spirit
    d. majority
    e. few

QUESTION   ANSWER

238. Jump is to leap as run is to . . .

    a. stop
    b. slow
    c. fast
    d. manage
    e. walk

QUESTION   ANSWER

239. House is to bricks as greenhouse is to . . .

    a. green
    b. clear
    c. glass
    d. plants
    e. shed

QUESTION   ANSWER

240.   Nib is to pen as pupil is to . . .

    a. teacher

    b. school

    c. eye

    d. colour

    e. iris

QUESTION   ANSWER

241.   Pig is to pork as deer is to . . .

    a. veal

    b. meat

    c. venison

    d. beef

    e. poultry

QUESTION   ANSWER

242.   West is to east as port is to . . .

    a. wine

    b. drink

    c. stern

    d. starboard

    e. hull

243. Fish is to water as bird is to . . .

    a. air
    b. glide
    c. fly
    d. wing
    e. beak

244. Weight is to kilogram as height is to . . .

    a. tall
    b. large
    c. fathom
    d. centimetre
    e. stretch

Word analogies 2

From the words presented below, circle the one that is the odd one out.

QUESTION	ANSWER

245.

    a. vodka
    b. whiskey
    c. brandy
    d. beer
    e. rum

QUESTION	ANSWER

246.

    a. superfluous
    b. unrelated
    c. extraneous
    d. excessive
    e. irrelevant

QUESTION	ANSWER

247.

    a. map
    b. plan
    c. address
    d. chart
    e. diagram

248.

    a. stall
    b. stop
    c. stand
    d. kiosk
    e. booth

249.

    a. tie
    b. knot
    c. fasten
    d. buckle
    e. strap

250.

    a. tip
    b. point
    c. end
    d. guide
    e. hint

QUESTION	ANSWER

251.

    a. liberty
    b. independence
    c. freedom
    d. permit
    e. autonomy

QUESTION	ANSWER

252.

    a. employ
    b. pay
    c. recompense
    d. compensate
    e. reward

QUESTION	ANSWER

253.

    a. leaf
    b. page
    c. sheet
    d. side
    e. book

QUESTION	ANSWER

254.

    a. time
    b. occasion
    c. moment
    d. instant
    e. immediately

QUESTION	ANSWER

255.

    a. plum
    b. lemon
    c. potato
    d. melon
    e. peach

QUESTION	ANSWER

256.

    a. tall
    b. high
    c. elevated
    d. lofty
    e. bold

QUESTION	ANSWER

257.

   a. Saturn
   b. Mercury
   c. Sun
   d. Mars
   e. Venus

QUESTION	ANSWER

258.

   a. mother
   b. father
   c. sister
   d. aunt
   e. grandmother

QUESTION	ANSWER

259.

   a. appropriate
   b. suitable
   c. fitting
   d. bereft
   e. proper

QUESTION	ANSWER

260.

    a. anxiety
    b. concern
    c. nerve
    d. worry
    e. fear

QUESTION	ANSWER

261.

    a. arid
    b. dry
    c. scorched
    d. baked
    e. stale

QUESTION	ANSWER

262.

    a. usual
    b. ordinary
    c. regular
    d. habit
    e. normal

QUESTION	ANSWER

263.

   a. promote
   b. denigrate
   c. sell
   d. advertise
   e. market

QUESTION	ANSWER

264.

   a. perspective
   b. view
   c. opinion
   d. outlook
   e. potential

Practice websites

If you feel you want to practise more with word analogy tests, there are a few websites from which you can access practice tests for free:

http://www.queendom.com/mindgames/mindstretching/iq_quizzes/
   iq-quiz17.html
http://www.rhlschool.com/eng3n29.htm
http://www.rhlschool.com/eng3n33.htm

Text comprehension

The type of verbal reasoning test that you are most likely to face in a recruitment situation, especially for graduate or managerial positions, is a text comprehension test. This verbal reasoning test is designed to assess your ability to reason with information given in a short passage, followed by a number of statements.

There are two types of text comprehension test, and they differ in the way in which you are required to respond to the statements. The first type requires you to respond to each statement by indicating whether it is True, False or Cannot Say, based on the information in the passage. The second type presents you with several statements (typically four), and you have to decide which of them is most true, again based on the information in the passage.

What topics can the passages be on?

There are no firm rules about what topics the passages refer to, but they generally avoid sensitive topics. This means that subjects such as religion and politics or those that refer to discrimination or are morbid are not used. Apart from that, a passage could be on any non-offensive topic, from an item on the parking regulations in Central London to a piece on the effects of climate change in Canada.

This means that you are likely to be faced with a topic of which you have no prior knowledge. However, this is more likely to be an advantage than a disadvantage because you are required to respond to the statements based solely on the information presented to you in the passage and not on previous knowledge. Having previous knowledge of the topic in a passage could, in fact, lead you to make wrong assumptions.

Are there rules underlying the statements?

There are no specific rules governing the way in which the statements in text comprehension tests are created. A True statement could simply be a paraphrase of a sentence from the passage, or it could be a statement that can be definitely inferred from something stated within a sentence. True statements could also be simply a combination of information from two parts of the passage or an implication that can be assumed based on two or more statements in the passage. There are several points that can help you get the right answer.

Watch out for distracters

You have to be aware that the people who design the tests do not focus only on creating the question and the correct answer. They are also thinking about the remaining multiple-choice options they give. These are called distracters because they are designed to distract you – that is, they look as if they are the correct answer when they are not. There are several ways in which a distracter can be created in verbal reasoning tests, and although they will depend on the individual test designer, there are several ways in which distracters are usually created, so it would be useful for you to be aware of them.

An option could paraphrase a statement but overemphasize a detail, thus making it incorrect. For example, you should be suspicious of words such as 'always', 'never', 'all', 'none', 'only' and 'solely'. If these words are included in a paraphrased statement when the actual passage does not imply them, the statement will be either False or Cannot Say. This means that you must pay attention to detail when you are completing a text comprehension test, because the difference between a True and a False statement could be just one word.

A distracter can also take the form of a paraphrase of a sentence with a detail that is not included in the text, thus making the statement incorrect.

Sometimes a distracter makes an assumption that is based on common sense but that cannot definitely be inferred from the passage. For example, a passage could state that a painter was Italian, and one of the options could be that the painter created his works of art in Italy. Although this statement could be true, and is highly likely based on common sense, you cannot definitely infer that a painter will have necessarily created his artwork in his place of origin.

Similarly, be aware of assumptions that are based on previous knowledge but that cannot definitely be inferred from the passage.

Distracters sometimes include the word 'equally'. A passage might talk about a common effect of two things, for example, but this does not mean that their effect is equal. 'Mainly' is another word to be cautious about. If a sentence is structured in a way that more emphasis seems to be given to one factor, this does not mean that this is necessarily the main factor.

Although the above guidelines will be useful in alerting you to most distracters, you should bear in mind that they are not infallible. For example, if you see a 'never' in a statement, do not immediately dismiss it as a distracter. There is always the possibility that the passage actually implied that the statement is true. Take care to focus on the details when you see this type of statement. There is a high probability that it will be a distracter, but you must always double-check.

True, false and 'Cannot Say' questions

Based on the information presented in the following passages, state whether each statement is true, false or 'Cannot Say'.

Passage 1

In vertebrates bone is constantly being formed and broken down throughout life. The body contains cells that replenish bone, called osteoblasts, and also cells that continuously degrade it, called osteoclasts. In an ideal situation, the action of these two types of cell is perfectly balanced, allowing the bone to maintain bone mass. If this balance is upset and more bone is destroyed than formed, osteoporosis may develop. Scientists have recently discovered a way to trigger bone production, raising hopes for a treatment for osteoporosis. A research team found that it could massively increase bone mass in mice by altering the structure of a protein in the body. The modification is so minor that they hope the side-effects will be minimal if the process is repeated in humans.

STATEMENTS	ANSWER (T/F/CS)
265. The body typically has an equal number of cells that degrade and that replenish bone.	
266. Osteoporosis is due to more bone being replenished than is degraded.	
267. Osteoporosis is caused by the malfunctioning of a protein in the body.	
268. Bone is replenished at a lower rate as vertebrates get older.	

Passage 2

A research team has suggested that a particular gene may make some people susceptible to drug addiction. Brain cells contain a type of receptor called 'mu opioid receptors', which can allow drug molecules to bind to the brain. If these receptors are abnormal, they allow more drug and alcohol molecules to bind to the brain than usual, and this can lead to drug addiction. In laboratory studies the team observed a genetic variation that can make the mu opioid receptors much more vulnerable to the effects of addictive drugs. According to the researchers, this finding means that one day they may be able to tailor treatments for addiction according to the way a person's genes behave.

STATEMENTS	ANSWER (T/F/CS)

269. According to the research team, all addictions have a genetic basis.

270. A genetic variation may cause an increase in mu opioid receptors, which can cause addiction.

271. Mu opiod receptors allow molecules of drugs and alcohol to bind to brain cells.

272. The purpose of this research was to investigate whether treatments could one day be individually tailored.

Passage 3

A tropical cyclone is a large, rotating system of clouds, wind and thunderstorm activity. The factors that lead to a tropical cyclone can include a pre-existing weather disturbance, warm tropical oceans, moisture and no more than light winds. The primary energy source of a tropical cyclone is the release of large amounts of heat as moist air is carried upwards and its water vapour condenses. If the right conditions persist for long enough, they can combine to produce the violent winds, waves, rain and floods associated with this phenomenon. While cyclones can be highly destructive, they are an important part of the atmospheric circulation system, which moves heat from the equatorial region towards the higher latitudes.

STATEMENTS	ANSWER (T/F/CS)
273. A tropical cyclone cannot form if there is no wind.	
274. The condensation of water vapour is typically necessary to maintain a tropical cyclone.	
275. Tropical cyclones are as beneficial as they are destructive for the environment.	
276. A tropical cyclone moves heat from higher to lower latitudes.	

Passage 4

Sleep apnoea is a sleep disorder in which a person stops breathing during sleep because their airway closes. As the brain senses the build-up of carbon dioxide that results from the blocked airway, it activates muscles that open the airway. This allows breathing to resume but at the same time interrupts sleep. Studies suggest that this disorder occurs in 1–2 per cent of middle-aged men and in approximately half that number of women. One method of treatment is with nasal Continuous Positive Airway Pressure (CPAP), which is a machine that delivers air to the throat, preventing the airway from becoming blocked. Although initial research showed no benefits of the use of CPAP, recent controlled studies have demonstrated the efficacy of the technique.

STATEMENTS	ANSWER (T/F/CS)
277. In sleep apnoea the blocked airway is opened in response to the accumulation of carbon dioxide.	
278. People who suffer from sleep apnoea can never enjoy uninterrupted sleep.	
279. Women are more likely to suffer from sleep apnoea when they are middle-aged.	
280. Until recently there was evidence both for and against the effectiveness of CPAP as a treatment for sleep apnoea.	

Passage 5

The principal technique for the genetic modification of plants uses the natural ability of a bacterium that infects plants. The bacterium transfers a piece of its own DNA into the DNA of the infected plant. This DNA causes the plant to form a tumour-like growth called a crown gall. This houses the bacteria and produces nutrients that support their growth. A number of scientists contributed to this discovery throughout the late 1960s and the 1970s. By 1983 biotechnology had reached the point where it was possible to insert additional beneficial genes into the bacterium and thus transfer those genes into plants.

STATEMENTS	ANSWER (T/F/CS)
281. The transfer of a bacterium's DNA to a plant is always harmful for the plant when it occurs naturally.	
282. The bacterium causes the plant cell to create a tumour-like growth, from which it will subsequently feed.	
283. Genetically modified plants have been created only by utilizing the ability of bacteria to transfer DNA.	
284. Scientists have been investigating techniques for genetic modification since the 1960s.	

Passage 6

A lottery-linked deposit account (LLDA) is one whereby a depositor receives one chance each month to win a prize for every monetary unit they hold in the deposit account, where the monetary unit varies according to the specific LLDA. The lottery does not affect the value of the deposit but rather the interest rate that the holder receives. The total interest is the same as for an equivalent deposit account, but it is used to create a lottery prize fund that is distributed only among the few lucky winners.

STATEMENTS	ANSWER (T/F/CS)
285. In any given month an LLDA will offer most people a lower interest than a normal deposit account.	
286. The principal of an LLDA is that depositors risk losing the money that they save to win a big prize.	
287. LLDAs generally pay out less in total interest across all savers than a normal deposit account.	
288. In a whole year a depositor typically makes as much from prizes as they would from interest in an equivalent deposit account.	

Passage 7

Despite 36 months of falling unemployment and some improvement in educational qualifications throughout the UK, the proportion of people unemployed or living in low-income households in the north is still slightly higher than it was five years ago. The latest available figures show that the number of children in these households has not changed for a decade, in contrast to the rest of the country, where it has declined year on year.

	STATEMENTS	ANSWER (T/F/CS)
289.	Proportionally fewer people in the north were unemployed or living in low-income households five years ago.	
290.	More people were unemployed in the north last year than are unemployed now.	
291.	Outside of the north, unemployment has not fallen over the last year.	
292.	Outside of the north, there are fewer children living in low-income households than last year.	

Passage 8

While inflation is a government's way of paying for projects without explicitly taxing its citizens, it is no less burdensome. Inflation occurs when a government creates more money, which results in a decrease in people's purchasing power. The chief impetus for a government to encourage inflation is a desire to spend more than it takes in. In effect, inflation helps borrowers at the expense of lenders. This consequently is beneficial for the public sector, which is a net borrower, and detrimental for the private sector, which is a net lender.

STATEMENTS	ANSWER (T/F/CS)
293. In situations of high inflation it is financially more advantageous to be a lender than a borrower.	
294. Inflation is another tax on a country's citizens.	
295. The public and private sectors borrow similar amounts in any given year.	
296. A government generally encourages inflation to allow it to spend more money than it collects.	

Passage 9

On discovering any fire, immediately activate the building fire alarm system. This will automatically notify the fire department. It will also sound the fire alarm bells and shut down the air-handling units to prevent the spread of smoke. It is better to have the fire department respond and not be needed than to have them arrive too late for a potential rescue. If the fire is small enough, use the correct type of fire extinguisher to control it. Do not fight a fire if you don't know what is burning; if you don't have the correct extinguisher; if the fire might block your escape route; or if you begin to inhale smoke. If the first attempts to put out the fire do not succeed, evacuate the building immediately without using elevators.

	STATEMENTS	ANSWER (T/F/CS)
297.	The fire alarm serves three specific purposes.	
298.	Having a false alarm for a fire is preferable to not sounding the alarm when a fire is suspected.	
299.	If a fire is small you should fight it with the first ire extinguisher that you find.	
300.	The fire department will not mind being called out to a false alarm.	

Passage 10

It is anticipated that approximately 60 grants will be offered for students from sub-Saharan Africa in 2007–2008. The number of these annual grants has augmented somewhat in recent years by the awarding of several Islamic civilization grants for projects in this region. These are grants designed to enhance the knowledge and understanding of Islam and of Islamic history and culture. The year 2006 was particularly noteworthy in this regard, as a record six Islamic civilization grants have been awarded for these students. This represents 15 per cent of the Islamic civilization grants awarded worldwide that year.

STATEMENTS	ANSWER (T/F/CS)
301. The number of Islamic civilization grants awarded to students from sub-Saharan Africa varies from year to year.	
302. Islamic civilization grants are offered only to students from sub-Saharan Africa.	
303. Islamic civilization grants are primarily offered to Muslim students.	
304. More grants will be offered in 2007 than in 2006.	

Passage 11

Queen Anula of Sri Lanka is believed to have been the earliest known female monarch in Asia. She was also one of the first royal princesses to convert to Buddhism. She eventually succeeded her husband and served as co-ruler with four different kings. Historians believe that she was involved in a series of assassination plots, poisoning her husband Coranaga, who ruled for 12 years, and also her husband's other successor, Tissa.

	STATEMENTS	ANSWER (T/F/CS)
305.	Queen Anula succeeded her husband Tissa to the throne.	
306.	Queen Anula was one of the first people in Sri Lanka to become a Buddhist.	
307.	Queen Anula was the world's earliest known female monarch.	
308.	Queen Anula is believed to be responsible for the deaths of at least two kings.	

Passage 12

Konservat-lagerstätten are deposits of rock known for the exceptional preservation of fossilized organisms, where the soft parts are preserved in the form of impressions or casts. The mud that formed the deposits helped to prevent decay through the absence of oxygen that suppressed common bacterial decomposition long enough for the casts of soft body parts to form. Lagerstätten preserve soft-bodied organisms rather than the shells and bones that make up most of the fossil record, and therefore they offer a more complete record of ancient biodiversity and enable some reconstruction of the ecology of ancient aquatic communities. Konservat-lagerstätten are crucial in providing answers to important moments in the history and evolution of life – for example, the earliest known bird, archeopteryx, was found in the Solnhofen limestone deposits.

STATEMENTS	ANSWER (T/F/CS)
309. Konservat-lagerstätten allow us to have greater insight into the diversity of lifeforms available in the distant past.	
310. Most of the animals preserved in konservat-lagerstätten died from lack of oxygen.	
311. Archeopteryx is a good example of a Konservat-lagerstätten deposit.	
312. Only aquatic lifeforms are preserved in Konservat-lagerstätten deposits.	

Passage 13

A proposed amendment to the Irish constitution must first be formally approved by both houses of parliament, the Dáil and the Senate, and then endorsed by the electorate in a referendum. A simple majority in this vote is sufficient to approve an amendment, and there is no minimum turn-out required for a constitutional referendum to be considered valid. The vote occurs by secret ballot. Although UK citizens resident in Ireland may vote in a general election, only Irish citizens can participate in a referendum. After being approved by referendum, an amendment must be signed into law by the president. This is a mere formality because, provided the correct procedure has been complied with, the president cannot veto an amendment.

	STATEMENTS	ANSWER (T/F/CS)
313.	A majority of Irish citizens must agree for an amendment to be approved in a referendum.	
314.	The president has never disagreed with an amendment to the constitution.	
315.	Only Irish citizens can vote in general elections in Ireland.	
316.	An amendment should be approved by the Dáil, the Senate and by the electorate before it can be signed into law.	

Passage 14

The *naumachia* was a re-enactment of naval battles. The first known *naumachia* was given by Julius Caesar to celebrate his quadruple triumph in 46 BC. He had an artificial basin dug near the River Tiber capable of holding actual ships, and had 2,000 combatants and 4,000 rowers fight an actual sea battle. The *naumachia* was bloodier than gladiatorial games, which consisted of smaller engagements where the combat did not necessarily end with the death of the losers. The *naumachia* could represent historical or pseudo-historical themes. Each of the fleets participating represented a maritime power. It required significantly greater resources than other such entertainments, and as such these spectacles were reserved for exceptional occasions, closely tied to celebrations of the emperor, his victories and his monuments.

STATEMENTS	ANSWER (T/F/CS)
317. The *naumachia* did not necessarily end with the death of the losers.	
318. The costs of staging a *naumachia* were so high that they were reserved for very special occasions.	
319. Most *naumachias* had at least 2,000 combatants and a greater number of rowers.	
320. A *naumachia* was usually accompanied by some gladiatorial games.	

Passage 15

A honeybee that is away foraging will rarely sting, except when stepped on or handled roughly. Honeybees only actively sting when they perceive their hive to be threatened, often being alerted by the release of attack pheromones. Although it is widely believed that a worker honeybee can sting only once, this is a misconception. The bee's stinger evolved for combat between bees of different hives, and the barbed stinger can still penetrate another bee's exoskeleton and retract safely. However, if the bee stings a mammal, the stinger becomes lodged in the mammal's skin and it will tear loose from the bee's abdomen and lead to her death in minutes.

	STATEMENTS	ANSWER (T/F/CS)
321.	Most bees are female.	
322.	A honeybee can sting a human only once.	
323.	The bee's stinger developed to allow the release of attack pheromones.	
324.	Mammals are rarely stung by honeybees.	

Passage 16

Only two species of camel exist today: the Bactrian camel and the dromedary camel. The former has two humps and is native to Asia, whereas the latter has only one hump and is native to North and East Africa. Bactrian camels have thick, long, warm, shaggy coats in winter and are equipped for very extreme temperatures. They can withstand cold down to minus 40°C, but in summer they shed their coats and can stand temperatures up to 50°C. Dromedary camels have only a short fibre coat, even in winter, and they are typically taller than Bactrian camels at the humps. Dromedary camels are not equipped for the degree of cold that Bactrian camels can withstand.

	STATEMENTS	ANSWER (T/F/CS)
325.	Dromedary camels can withstand extremes of temperatures.	
326.	Dromedary camels shed their coats in summer.	
327.	There are no Bactrian camels in Africa.	
328.	Camels that are shorter at the humps are native to Asia.	

Passage 17

A bongo is a small drum that is often made of wood or metal with a layer of animal skin stretched across the top. It is common for two of these drums to be held together with a thick piece of wood. The drums are then held between the knees and traditionally played using the fingers to strike the drums. Bongo drums can be traced back to nineteenth-century Cuba, although examples with ceramic bodies can be found in Morocco, Egypt and other Middle Eastern countries. It is believed that the wooden drums are more commonly found in Cuba because they were originally brought there by the slave trade.

STATEMENTS	ANSWER (T/F/CS)
329. Bongo drums are played with the knees.	
330. Bongo drums found in Cuba are most likely to be made of wood.	
331. Bongos were around before 1900.	
332. Bongo drums do not exist in Morocco, Egypt or certain areas of the Middle East.	

Passage 18

The London Underground is an all-electric system of trains that run under the city of London in England. Despite the name, approximately 55 per cent of the system is actually above ground. It is the world's oldest underground railway system, with services commencing in January 1863, and it is also the world's largest in terms of route length. As of 2006, there were 275 stations with 3 million passenger journeys made each day. In 2004 and 2005 London Underground trains ran nearly 70 million kilometres in passenger service. In 2003 London Underground became part of Transport for London, which incorporates different forms of travel all across London, such as buses, overground trains, river boats and the Docklands Light Railway.

....

	STATEMENTS	ANSWER (T/F/CS)
333.	Before 1863 there was no underground railway system in the world.	
334.	Over half of the London Underground system is actually above the ground.	
335.	Over 3 million passengers travel on the London Underground every day.	
336.	The London Underground is formed of nearly 70 million kilometres of track.	

Passage 19

Maurits Cornelius Escher was a famous graphic artist. Born in 1898 in the Netherlands, he gave up his original vocation of architecture for graphic arts at the age of 21 years. His fascination with the subject followed from his first visit to an ancient mosque in Spain in 1922. Following extensive travels through Italy, he eventually married and moved to Rome in 1924, where he stayed until 1935, before moving to Switzerland. After two years he moved to Brussels, where he stayed for a further three years, eventually moving back to the Netherlands in 1941. During these later years, he published a paper called 'Regular Division of Plane', which discussed the role of symmetry and mathematics in art.

STATEMENTS	ANSWER (T/F/CS)
337. Escher was born in the Netherlands in the nineteenth century.	
338. Escher was living in Italy when he published the 'Regular Division of Plane'.	
339. Escher's first visit to the ancient mosque in Spain was before he was 21 years old.	
340. Escher got married in Italy.	

Passage 20

In the middle of the eighteenth century, macaroni was a term used to describe a fashionable male who dressed and spoke in an outlandishly affected manner. This was a derogatory term, and it also referred to people who drank and gambled excessively. The term derives from the Italian word *maccherone*, which means 'boorish fool' and was picked up by young men who visited Italy around this time. In fact, macaroni is the name given to a small tricorn hat, which is worn perched above a high wig, and this is an example of the eccentric clothes that macaroni fellows would wear.

STATEMENTS	ANSWER (T/F/CS)
341. The word 'macaroni' has more than one definition.	
342. Macaroni men existed before the eighteenth century.	
343. Macaroni is Italian for 'boorish fool'.	
344. A tricorn is a large, pointed hat placed on top of a wig.	

Multiple choice questions

Of the four statements presented, circle the one that is true, based on the information given in the passage.

Passage 1

The Swan Goose is a large goose with natural breeding grounds in Mongolia and eastern Russia. It is migratory and winters mainly in south and east China, where it is familiarly known as the Chinese Goose and has been domesticated for centuries. The Swan Goose has a long neck, a long black bill and a brown cap. Its upperparts are brown, and the legs are orange, though some populations are completely white. Some variants also have a bump on the top of the beak. This appears by 6–8 weeks of age and is more prominent in males.

....

345. STATEMENTS

    a. It is easy to distinguish between male and female Swan Geese.

    b. The Swan Goose gets its name from being a white goose.

    c. The Swan Goose originated from Mongolia

    d. The Swan Goose has been farmed in China for many years.

....

Passage 2

The Pangong Lake is situated in the Himalayas, at a height of about 4,250 metres. It is 134 kilometres long and extends from India to Tibet. Two-thirds of the length of this lake falls in the People's Republic of China. It is 5 kilometres wide at its broadest point. In winter the lake freezes completely, despite being filled with salt water. Pangong Lake is a five-hour drive from the Indian city of Leh, most of the drive being along a rough and dramatic mountain road that traverses the third-highest pass in the world.

346. STATEMENTS

    a. Pangong Lake is most easily accessed from India.

    b. The Pangong Lake is the third-highest lake in the world.

    c. The majority of the Pangong Lake is under Chinese control.

    d. It is unusual for a mountain lake to freeze.

Passage 3

According to a review of existing research that was published yesterday, the trend for children and adolescents to stay up later and sleep less may be linked to rising levels of obesity. The review highlighted that shortened sleeping times result in metabolic changes by altering the body's mechanisms that regulate appetite, which may contribute to obesity and diabetes. Limited sleep is a particular problem for teenagers, whose increased need for sleep is critical during adolescent years. Children who are tired are also less likely to engage in physical exercise, adding to the risk of weight increase.

347. STATEMENTS

    a. It is proposed that sleep loss causes obesity through multiple pathways.

    b. The findings are based on new experimental research.

    c. Younger children are more affected than teenagers by sleep loss.

    d. There is a clear link between sleep loss and diabetes.

Passage 4

Smenkhkare was a Pharaoh of the Eighteenth Dynasty, successor of Akhenaten and predecessor of Tutankhamun. He is thought to have ruled Egypt for two full years, from 1336 BC to 1334 BC, although his independent reign may have been as short as a few months. It is recorded that Tutankhamun's reign began immediately after Smenkhkare's death. The identity of Smenkhkare is somewhat mysterious, and it is not certain that he was a man. The difficulty is that Smenkhkare shares some names with Nefertiti, the wife of Akhenaten, and it is possible that they are the same person.

....

348. STATEMENTS
   a. Smenkhkare lived during Akhenaten's reign as Pharaoh.
   b. Smenkhkare ruled Egypt for at least two years.
   c. Smenkhkare was the wife of Akhenaten.
   d. Tutankhamun was the eighteenth Pharaoh of Egypt.

....

Passage 5

Cleopatra's Needles are a trio of obelisks in London, Paris and New York City. Each is carved from red granite, stands about 21 metres high, weighs about 180 tons and is inscribed with Egyptian hieroglyphs. Although the Needles are genuine Ancient Egyptian obelisks, they are somewhat misnamed as none has any connection with Queen Cleopatra VII of Egypt. They were originally erected in the Egyptian city of Heliopolis around 1450 BC, though the inscriptions were added about 200 years later to commemorate the military victories of Ramses II.

....

349. STATEMENTS
   a. Cleopatra ruled Egypt in the period around 1450 BC.
   b. The Cleopatra's Needle in London is unchanged from when it was originally created.
   c. The three Cleopatra's Needles are identical.
   d. There are only three 'Cleopatra Needles'.

....

Passage 6

It has been said that half of each company's spending on advertising is wasted, and for some companies the level of wastage could be even more. Nonetheless, last year the leading national advertisers increased their advertising expenditure by 9 per cent. Given the expense, companies are keen to improve the efficiency of their advertising – that is, the ratio of sales attributed to expenditure. Despite the common belief that the money spent on media advertising is not being used optimally, there is currently no easy way to measure the possible inefficiency or the potential sales losses due to inefficient use of advertising expenditure.

350. STATEMENTS

a. Since last year the expenditure on advertising has increased by 9 per cent.

b. Most leading national advertisers believe that their advertising expenditure is wasted.

c. It is currently difficult to identify where advertising money is best spent.

d. Many companies are keen to increase their advertising in order to improve sales.

Passage 7

Rabies is a disease caused by the Lyssa virus, which, among other things, attacks the nervous system and can cause encephalitis, which is inflammation of the brain. Although it is known as a disease that infects dogs, it can affect all warm-blooded creatures, including man. People are most often infected by the bite of a dog, bat or monkey, though in Europe the virus is mainly carried by the fox. Normally, the onset of symptoms occurs between one and three months after infection. Once visible symptoms have developed, the mortality rate is almost 100 per cent. However, rabies can be prevented with a vaccine, and even if a person has been infected, the disease can be treated before the symptoms develop.

351. STATEMENTS
   a. An animal or a human that has been infected by rabies will also suffer from encephalitis.
   b. Outside Europe rabies most frequently infects dogs.
   c. The Lyssa virus can infect only warm-blooded creatures.
   d. The treatment of rabies is rarely effective after three months of infection.

Passage 8

In economics the study of consumption investigates how and why society and individuals consume goods and services and how this affects society and human relationships. In the last ten years economic research has focused on the role of consumption in creating people's identity and the 'consumer society'. However, traditionally consumption was seen as rather unimportant compared to the production of goods, and the political and economic issues surrounding it. With the development of a consumer society and increasing consumer power in the marketplace, the economics of consumption have become recognized as central to modern life. Companies and academics aim to use the study of consumption to inform marketing strategy, improve product design and product branding as well as economic theory.

....

352. STATEMENTS

    a. Early research into economics considered the role of people's identity.

    b. Companies have a greater interest than academics in studying the economics of consumption.

    c. Interest in the economics of consumption has increased alongside the growth of the 'consumer society'.

    d. The importance of consumer economics has remained unchanged for the last decade.

....

Passage 9

Inductive reasoning is the process of arriving at a conclusion based on a set of observations, but in itself it is not a valid method of proof. Because a person observes a number of situations in which a pattern exists does not mean that that pattern is true for all situations. For example, after seeing many people outside with umbrellas, one may observe that every person who uses a purple umbrella is female. In turn, one could falsely conclude that only females use purple umbrellas. Inductive reasoning is useful for forming ideas about complex and real-life situations and generating hypotheses that can be investigated through more formal scientific research to determine whether they are right, wrong or only partially wrong.

....

353. STATEMENTS

    a. Observation is a valid method for proving a hypothesis.

    b. Inductive reasoning is important for focusing scientific research.

    c. Valid methods of scientific proof do not require inductive reasoning.

    d. Inductive reasoning is more useful for exploring complex rather than simple situations.

....

Passage 10

The blue iguana is the world's rarest lizard, with the wild population expected to be extinct within ten years. However, conservationists are celebrating success because, for the first time, eggs laid by a captive-bred Grand Cayman blue iguana, which had been released into a nature reserve on the Caribbean island, have successfully hatched. Since 2004 219 iguanas have been bred in captivity, being released into the wild once they are large enough not to be eaten by snakes in an attempt to save the critically endangered species. This programme is in response to the halving of this natural habitat of the iguana in the previous ten years, resulting in the wild population decreasing by 80 per cent.

354. STATEMENTS

    a. The blue iguana can be found only on Grand Cayman Island.

    b. The breeding programme involves releasing hatchling iguanas into the wild.

    c. It is due to predatory snakes that the world's rarest lizard is close to extinction.

    d. It is hoped that releasing iguanas bred in captivity will prevent them from becoming extinct in the wild.

Passage 11

London Bridge crosses the River Thames between Cannon Street Railway Bridge and Tower Bridge. On the south side of the bridge is London Bridge train station, and to the north is the Monument to the Great Fire of London. At least five London Bridges have existed at this site over the past 2,000 years, with the current bridge being opened in 1973. The previous bridge was sold to an American businessman for nearly $12.5 million in 1968. This bridge was reconstructed and now stands in Arizona at Lake Havasu City.

355. STATEMENTS

a. Cannon Street Railway Bridge is to the east of London Bridge.

b. The original London Bridge is now in Arizona.

c. The current London Bridge has been standing for over 30 years.

d. The reconstructed London Bridge in Arizona is currently worth $12.5 million.

Passage 12

Bengal tigers are native to Asia and live in a wide range of climates across the continent. They are most common in India and Bangladesh. Males are longer than females, averaging 2.9 metres from head to tail, compared to only 2.5 metres for females. They are also the heavier of the species, weighing approximately 220 kilograms. Bengal tigers usually prey on wild animals, such as deer, cattle, pigs and buffaloes, and the size of their territory varies according to the availability of prey. Although most tigers are orange with black stripes, white tigers are occasionally sighted. These are a colour variation of Bengal tigers rather than a separate species. However, their actual frequency is unknown, with only about twelve sightings within the last century.

....

356. STATEMENTS
   a. Female Bengal tigers weigh approximately 220 kilograms.
   b. Bengal tigers only eat wild animals.
   c. All Bengal tigers are white in colour.
   d. The size of a Bengal tiger's territory depends on the availability of prey.

....

Passage 13

An amphitheatre is a public building of the Roman period once used for spectator sports, games and great displays. The largest and most famous of these is the Colosseum in Rome. This is also known as the Flavian amphitheatre after the dynasty that built it, and it could seat almost 50,000 spectators. Another well-preserved amphitheatre is located in El Djem, Tunisia. This could seat up to 35,000 spectators and remained more or less intact until the seventeenth century. Often incorrectly called a colosseum, the ruins at El Djem were declared a World Heritage Site in 1979.

....

357. STATEMENTS

    a. Amphitheatres were used for spectator sports and games until the seventeenth century.

    b. The Colosseum in Rome is a World Heritage Site.

    c. There are no amphitheatres in the world that could seat more than 50,000 people.

    d. The Flavian amphitheatre is located in Tunisia.

....

Passage 14

A bascule bridge opens upwards, like a drawbridge. The term 'bascule' is French for seesaw and balance, and this is the principle that bascule bridges employ: a counterweight balances the weight of the bridge throughout its upward swing, which allows boat traffic to pass under it. Bascule bridges are the most common type of movable bridge in existence today because they are quick to operate and require little energy. A good example of a bascule bridge is Tower Bridge in London, which crosses the River Thames. Originally built as a hydraulically operated bridge using steam from coal-burning boilers to power the bascule engines, the bascule mechanism is now driven by oil and electricity.

....

358. STATEMENTS

    a. In a bascule bridge the weight of the bridge is similar to that of the counterweight.

    b. Tower Bridge is now powered by steam from coal-burning boilers.

    c. There are more bascule bridges in existence than any other type of bridge.

    d. A counterweight is used to control the bridge as it completes its downwards swing.

....

Passage 15

Bonsai is the art of growing miniature trees in containers. Bonsai trees are the same as full-size trees growing in the wild, but they are kept small by pruning both the leaves and the roots. Different tree species require different types of pruning; however, some pruning must be done only in the proper season. This is because most trees go through a period without growing any new roots or leaves, and inappropriate pruning can cause the tree to weaken or die. To shape the trees throughout the year, copper or aluminium wire can be wrapped around the trunks and branches of most species and bent to the desired shape. However, once this has been achieved, the wire should be removed.

....

359. STATEMENTS

    a. Bonsai trees should be pruned only once a year.

    b. Wire should be placed around the trunk and branches of a bonsai tree to restrict its growth.

    c. The leaves of the bonsai should be pruned at a different time from the roots.

    d. Not all bonsai trees grow new roots and leaves during the same season.

....

Passage 16

The United Nations Security Council is charged with maintaining peace and security among nations. While other organizations of the United Nations only make recommendations to member governments, the Security Council has the power to make decisions that member governments must carry out under the UN Charter. The Security Council is made up of 15 member states, consisting of five permanent seats and ten temporary seats. The permanent five members hold veto power over substantive but not procedural resolutions. The ten temporary seats are held for two-year terms, with member states voted in by the UN General Assembly on a regional basis. The presidency of the Security Council is rotated alphabetically each month.

....

360. STATEMENTS

   a. Each of the temporary members of the UN Security Council will serve as president at least twice during their two-year term.
   b. Temporary members have the power to veto procedural but not substantive resolutions.
   c. The UN Security Council has the power to force governments to carry out its decisions.
   d. All the members of the UN Security Council are voted in by the UN General Assembly.

....

Passage 17

Frankincense is an aromatic resin used in incense as well as in perfumes. It is tapped from boswellia trees through slashing the bark and allowing the exuded resin to harden and then be extracted. Tapping is performed two or three times a year, with the final taps producing the best resin because of their higher aromatic terpene content. High-quality resin can be visually discerned through its higher level of opacity. Omani frankincense is said to be the best resin in the world and is particularly milky in colour.

361. STATEMENTS

a. Frankincense is hard when it is harvested from the boswellia tree.

b. Omani frankincense is known for its transparent appearance.

c. Tapping is performed every four or every six months.

d. Boswellia trees are also known as frankincense trees.

Passage 18

A national anthem is generally a patriotic musical composition that evokes and eulogizes the history, traditions and struggles of a nation. Anthems rose to prominence in Europe during the nineteenth century. Due to European colonial influence, many non-European nations were influenced to adopt a European-style national anthem, with just a few having anthems rooted in indigenous traditions. The majority of national anthems are either marches or hymns, while a handful of countries use a simple fanfare. Anthems by their nature have to be brief, with the average being about one minute in length. However, most manage to be a true representation of the nation's musical character. South Africa's national anthem is unique in that five of the eleven official languages are used in the same anthem.

....

362. STATEMENTS
      a. South Africa is the only country to have a national anthem in more than two languages.
      b. Very few anthems are more than one minute long.
      c. Not all national anthems are sung.
      d. There were only a few national anthems outside Europe in the nineteenth century.

....

Passage 19

A ghost train is a funfair ride, designed primarily for children. Typically, it consists of a train that moves quite slowly through a darkened tunnel decorated with horror-related items, such as models of skeletons, witches and ghosts. 'Spooky' music and/or sound-effects will usually be played during the ride. Typically one or more of the models will be moved by hydraulics, or some other mechanism, when the train passes by. For example, a skeleton may sit up in a coffin or a ghost may fly past.

363. STATEMENTS
   a. Ghost trains are designed to terrify children.
   b. Most ghost trains work using electrified tracks.
   c. Most ghost trains rides are quite short in length.
   d. Despite having the same basic elements, ghost trains can differ on specific elements.

Passage 20

Etching is a method of engraving in which lines or textures are bitten, or etched, with acid into a metal plate. The image produced has a spontaneity of line that comes from drawing on the plate in the same direct way as with pen or pencil on paper. The first etchings date from the early sixteenth century, but the basic principle had been used earlier for the decoration of armour. Among the pioneers of the medium were Albrecht Altdorfer, Albrecht Dürer and Parmigianino; the greatest of all etchers was Rembrandt. In the twentieth century, etching was especially popular for book illustration.

----

364. STATEMENTS

   a. Before the sixteenth century, etching had been used only for the decoration of armour.

   b. Etching was not used by the Ancient Romans.

   c. Etching was particularly popular among German and Dutch painters.

   d. A pen or pencil is used to produce the image used in etching.

----

5 Abstract reasoning tests

Abstract reasoning tests assess your ability to identify patterns within diagrams. The questions consist of diagrams that follow certain rules, and what you need to do is understand these rules. That is all there is to it. They do not contain any numerical or verbal information and therefore do not require any prior learning for you to solve them.

Below is a typical example of an abstract reasoning question. There are five boxes in a row, four of which contain a pattern and one of which is empty. The question is, 'Which is the missing diagram?' Because this is not a test of your drawing ability, you will always be presented with a number of diagrams, from which you have to choose the correct one.

1 x 5 type

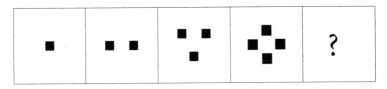

The following is another typical example of an abstract reasoning question. This consists of four boxes, three of which include a diagram and one of which is empty. The question however is the same, 'Which is the missing diagram?' and again you will be presented with diagrams from which you have to choose the correct one.

2 x 2 type

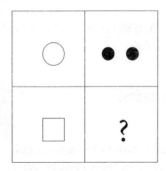

Another way in which abstract reasoning questions can be presented is in nine boxes, eight of which include a diagram and one of which is empty. The question again is, 'Which is the missing diagram?'

3 x 3 type

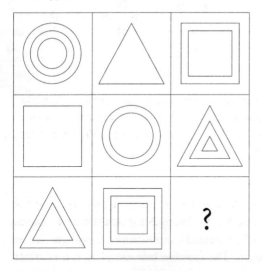

As you can see, the diagrams can be presented in different formats, and the questions that are posed could be of a different format from the 4-, 5- or 9-box format you have just seen. However, the steps that you need to follow to solve abstract reasoning tests are the same, no matter how the diagrams are presented.

After you have finished going through this section, you will see that they are not as hard as you might have thought.

How do you solve abstract reasoning questions?

Solving an abstract reasoning problem can be broken down into small, easily followed steps. You will not need to learn these steps by heart because after you have solved a few practice questions you will be able to solve the questions without having to think about them.

Let's work with the 5-box example that was shown earlier.

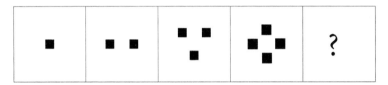

Step 1
Observe. Look at the patterns presented and ask yourself, 'What do I see?' Don't worry about it: no one knows you are having a silent discussion with yourself, so feel free to answer, 'I see 1 dot, then 2 dots, then 3 dots, then 4 dots.'

Step 2
Think. Now ask yourself, 'What is the rule behind what I see?' The rule seems to be that each box has one more dot than the box on its left. This rule will work if you look at the boxes from left to right. If you looked at the boxes from right to left the rule would be that each box has one fewer dot than the box on its right. No matter which way you look at the diagrams, the underlying rules are the same for the 1 x 5 type questions.

Step 3

Apply. Once you have worked out the rules, all you have to do is apply them to get to the correct answer. When you know that each box has one more dot than the box on its left and that the box on the left of the empty box has 4 dots, you will be know that the empty box should have 5 dots.

Step 4

Identify. You know what the answer should look like, so all you need to do is look at the options you are given, and find the one that matches the rule you have worked out.

Unfortunately, it is unlikely that the questions you get will be this simple, but although the diagrams will have more complex shapes, and the solution will not be so obvious, the rule will be simple.

TIP: Although it doesn't matter which way you look at a 1 x 5 type question, this is not always the case for a 2 x 2 or a 3 x 3 type question. In these cases, the underlying rule could be across rows or across columns. If the rule is across rows, each cell is related to the cell to its left (and right). If the rule is across columns, each cell is related to the cell above (or below). Don't worry if you can't picture it, it will become clear when you go through the examples in the following section.

Note also that with 2 x 2 and 3 x 3 type questions you will come across examples that have rules both across rows and across columns. This does not mean that you have to work harder to answer these questions. It actually means that you will have more information that will help you get to the solution, and less distracting information. If anything, it should be easier to solve these questions.

To keep things consistent, look at the examples in this section in the following order:

- 1 x 5 questions – from the box on the left towards the box on the right.

- 2 x 2 questions – on row 1, from the box on the left to the box on the right; then on row 2, from the box on the left to the box on the right.
- 3 x 3 questions – row 1, from the box on the left towards the box on the right; on row 2, from the box on the left towards the box on the right; on row 3, from the box on the left towards the box on the right.

Types of abstract reasoning questions

It would, of course, be great if specific rules were used to create abstract reasoning questions so that you would know what to look for, rather than having to work out everything from scratch every time. The good news is, there are! The majority of abstract reasoning questions are based on just a few rules, which will be explained in detail in the following sections.

TIP: When you are going through the different abstract reasoning questions you will probably be tempted to look immediately at the explanation directly beneath the question, especially when you come across a question that looks more difficult. However, many studies have shown that trying to solve a problem first and looking at its solution only when you are not able to solve it greatly increases your ability to solve similar problems. Therefore, if you want to learn how to solve abstract reasoning questions, rather than just observe how they are solved, you should always make an attempt to solve them.

Rule 1: Shapes added

The following abstract reasoning questions are based on the rule that shapes are added from one box to the next. The example of a 1 x 5 item that was discussed earlier was an example of shapes being added. Try to solve the following example, which is another question following the 'shapes added' rule.

....

365.

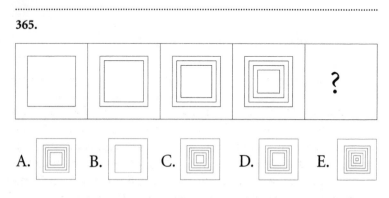

....

The logic in this question is that each box contains the same pattern as the square on its left, but has an extra square added in its interior. The correct answer is option C. Now try to solve the following question.

Although the explanations of the underlying logic will be given below each question, the answers will be included in the final chapter so that you do not see the answer before you work it out for yourself.

366.

A. B. C. D. E.

This question has the same underlying logic, 'shapes added', but each box contains the same number of shapes as the box on its left, plus one extra, rather than containing the same shapes, plus one extra. This makes the underlying logic less obvious by giving you information that you do not need to solve the question, and the aim is to make the question harder, even though the underlying rule is the same.

The following question is another example that follows the 'shapes added' logic.

367.

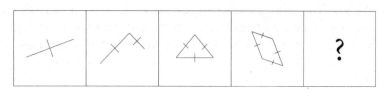

In this case the 'shape' that is added from one box to the next is a line, with a smaller vertical line cutting through it at its midpoint. What can be confusing in questions that add lines is that the lines can be interpreted as part of a shape rather than as separate lines, and this makes it harder to see the underlying rule.

Rule 2: Shapes subtracted

The following abstract reasoning questions are based on the rule that shapes are subtracted from one box to the next. Below is an example of such a question. Try to solve it before you look at the explanation.

368.

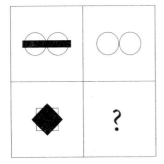

In this question each box on the right has the same shape as the box on its left but without the black shape – that is, the black shape is subtracted from one box to the next. This is an example of a 2 x 2 question, in which the rules work across rows.

There are several ways by which the 'shape subtracted' logic can be masked to make it is less obvious. Look, for example, at the question below:

369.

The rule that underlies this question is that each box contains one line fewer than the box on its left, but it also includes information that is intended to distract you from finding the answer. If you look at the first, second and fourth boxes, you might notice that the lines are parallel or perpendicular to each other, and this might lead you to waste time trying to work out whether the direction of the lines is relevant. However, the rule underlying this question is that, going from left to right, a line is subtracted.

Now look at the following question. It might at first look overwhelming, but remember the steps you need to follow – observe → think → apply → identify – and you can also take advantage of the fact that you already know that the rule is 'shapes subtracted'.

....

370.

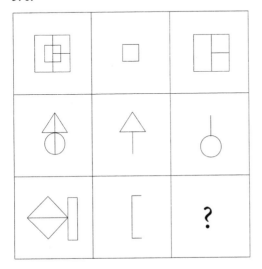

A. B. C. D. E.

....

This is an example of a 3 x 3 question, in which the rules are across rows rather than across columns. If you look closely at the first and the second boxes in each row you will see that the second box always contains a shape that is also present within the shape of the first box and then that the box on the right is what remains if you subtract the shapes that are in common from the first two boxes.

Rule 3: Shapes rotated

The following abstract reasoning questions are based on the rule that shapes are rotated in some way. Look at Question 371, which is an example of a 2 x 2 question following this rule.

....

371.

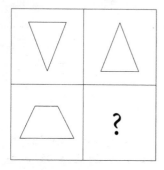

A.   B. C.   D. E.

....

Look at the boxes in the first row. From the first box to the second the shape is rotated by 180°. To find the missing shape in the second row you have to rotate the shape of the first box by 180°.

Now try to solve another example of such a question, presented in a 1 x 5 format:

....

372.

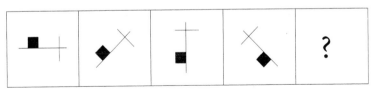

A. B. C. D. E.

....

Here, the shape is being rotated anticlockwise by 45°. Therefore, to find the shape for the last box, you need to rotate the shape 45° anti-clockwise.

Rule 4: Shapes split

The following questions are based on the rule that from one box to the next a shape is being split in some way. Consider, for example, Question 373.

....

373.

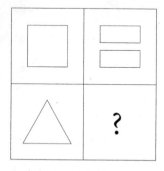

A. B. C. D. E.

....

This question follows the rule that from the box on the left to the box on the right the shape is split in half horizontally. To find the shape that is missing you need to split the triangle in half horizontally.

Rule 5: Shapes split and moved

A variation on the 'shapes split' rule is employed in the questions that follow. Question 374 is a 1 x 5 type question based on this variation.

374.

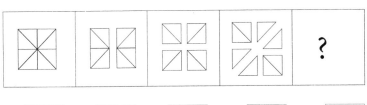

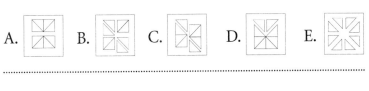

Although this is essentially a question that follows a 'shapes split' rule, it is obvious that the shapes are also moving – away from the line at which they were split. From left to right, the shape is first split horizontally, then vertically and then at one of the diagonals. The missing shape is the one that is split at the other diagonal.

Rule 6: Shapes merged and moved

Another variation on the 'shapes split' rule underlies some abstract reasoning questions. This time, however, the shapes are merged or moved in some way. Look at Question 375, which is similar to Question 374.

375.

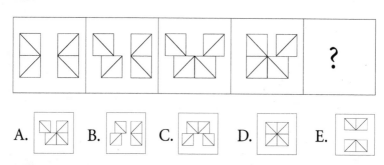

In order to work out the rule that underlies this question you should look at the relationships of the four small squares rather than at the shapes as a whole. You can see that from the first to the second box the bottom left square is moved towards the centre. From the second to the third box the bottom right square is moved towards the centre, and from the third to the fourth box the top left square is moved towards the centre. The fifth box, therefore, should contain the same shape as the fourth box, but with the top right square moved towards the centre.

TIP: You might have noticed that although it sometimes makes sense to look at certain shapes as a whole, the underlying rule might involve the individual parts that make up the shape. Question 375 was an example of this. Test developers occasionally use this rule to make a question more difficult, so if you can't make sense of a question's underlying rule when you are looking at the shapes, remember that the rule may relate to part or parts of the shapes rather than to the shapes as a whole.

Now look at the following question, which is an example of a 3 x 3 question that follows the 'shapes merged and moved' rule.

.....

376.

A. B. C. D. E.

.....

If you look at the boxes in the first row you can see that from the first to the second box the two shapes have merged or have moved towards the centre of the box. From the second to the third box, the shapes have moved in the same direction and by the same distance. The same rule underlies the shapes in the second row. When you look at the third row you can see how the shapes have moved from the first to the second box, so you need to apply the same rule to the second box, to give the answer.

Rule 7: Shade moved

Another variation on the 'shapes split and moved' rule is employed below.

....

377.

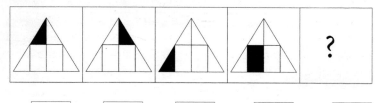

....

The question considers a triangle that has been divided into several sections. In each consecutive box, a different section is shaded. What rule determines which section is shaded? If you think about the shaded area as moving through the triangle, you'll see that it's progressing from left to right, first at the top of the triangle and then at the bottom. This should help you work out the next logical step.

Rule 8: Alternate shapes and patterns

Questions that follow the rule of 'alternate shapes and patterns' are essentially made up of a combination of different shapes with different patterns. Solve Question 378, for example..

....

378.

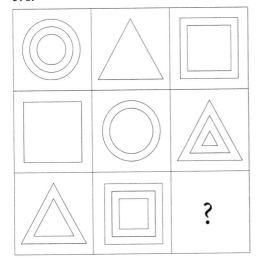

A. B. C. D. E.

....

There are essentially two rules underlying this question. The first is that each row contains a circle, a triangle and a square. The second is that a shape can be a single, double or triple shape. If you observe the shapes in the third row you will see that there are a double triangle and a triple square. So which one is missing?

Rule 9: Shapes altered

The shapes in questions based on this rule will change in different ways, but it is not usually difficult to identify the alteration, especially if you practise this type of question. Try to solve Question 379.

379.

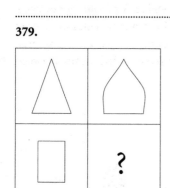

Rule 10: Symmetry

Finally, another rule that test devisers use is 'symmetry', and the patterns can be symmetrical in a number of ways. For example, a 1 x 5 item can be symmetrical around the middle box, while a 3 x 3 box can be symmetrical around the middle row, around the middle column or even around both simultaneously. This may sound complex, but it is often easier to observe symmetry than a different relationship between patterns. Consider Question 380.

380.

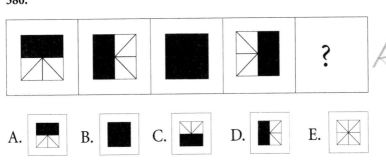

Once you understand that a question is following the symmetry rule, it is fairly easy to apply it to find the correct answer.

The rules outlined above are the ones that are most often used in abstract reasoning questions. This does not mean that these are the only rules that you may come across, of course, but even if you come across a rule that you haven't seen before, following the usual steps, observe → think → apply → identify, will allow you to get to the solution.

You should bear in mind that questions often involve a combination of rules rather than a single rule. Try to solve Question 381, for example.

381.

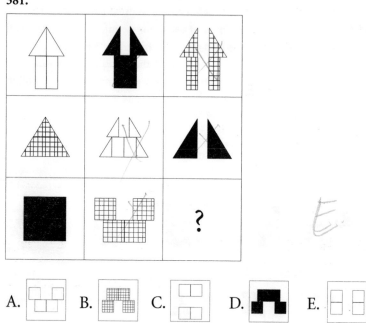

This question is based on two rules: it follows the 'shapes split and moved' rule and the 'alternate shapes and patterns' rule. Look at the first row. Each box contains essentially the same shape but, moving from left to right, you can see that the shape is split – first the top half is split, then the bottom half is split. In addition, the shape in each box has a different pattern. The same two rules can be applied to the second row. Therefore, if you apply these rules to the shapes in the third row you will get the correct answer.

Now that you have been through the different rules that underlie most abstract reasoning questions, all you have to do is practise them. The following pages contain practice questions that follow the rules described above and also various combinations of these rules.

Practice questions

In the questions that follow, find the shape that is missing.

382.

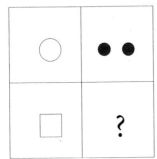

A. B. C. D. E.

383.

A. B. C. D. E.

384.

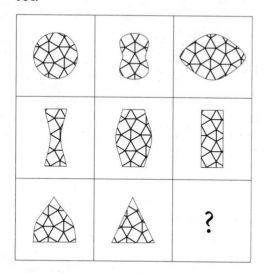

A.   B.   C.  D.   E.

385.

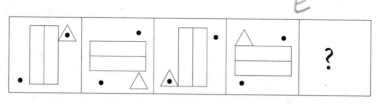

A.   B.   C.   D.   E.

386.

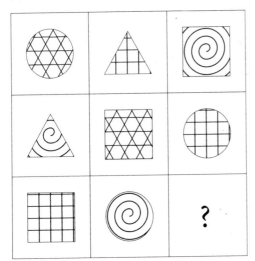

A. 　B. 　C. 　D. 　E.

387.

A. 　B. 　C. 　D. 　E.

388.

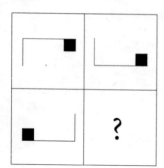

A. B. C.  D. E.

389.

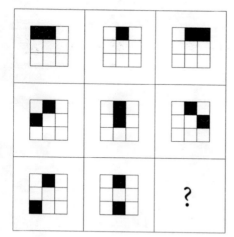

A. B. C. D. E.

390.

A. 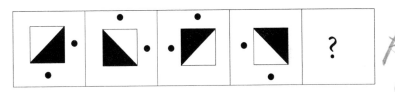 B. C. D. E.

391.

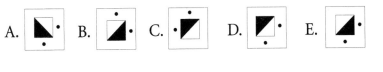

A. B. C. D. E.

392.

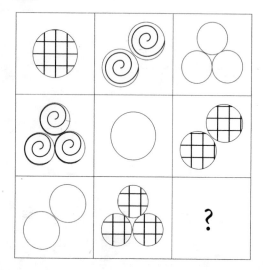

A. B. C. D. E.

393.

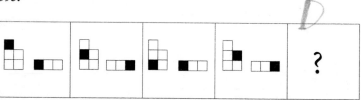

A. B. C.  D. E.

394.

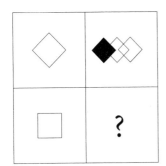

A. ■▥▥ B. ■▢▢ C. ◇◆ D. ■▢ E. ▢■

395.

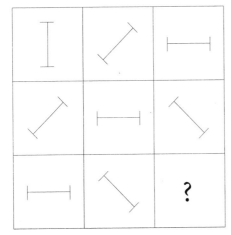

A. B. C. D. E.

396.

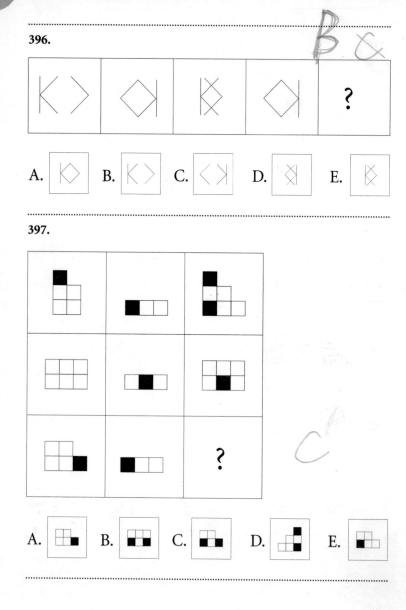

397.

398.

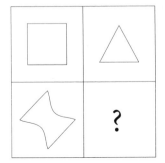

A. B. C. D. E.

399.

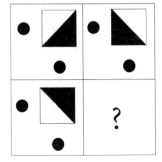

A. B. C. D. E.

400.

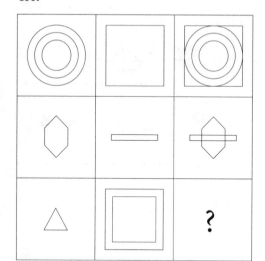

A. B. C. D.  E.

401.

A. B. C. D. E.

402.

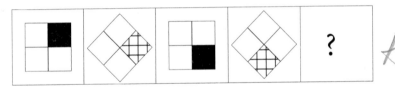

A. B. C. D. E.

403.

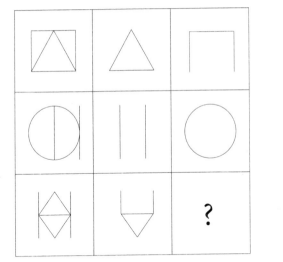

A. B. C. D. E.

404.

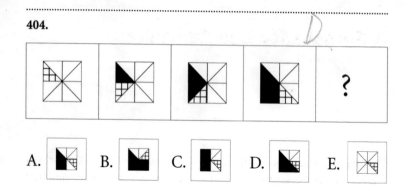

6 Personality questionnaires

Personality questionnaires are designed to assess a range of factors that are related to the way you tend to react to, and deal with, different situations. A lot of research has been carried out into which factors have the greatest effect on personality, but no conclusive results have been found. Most researchers, however, agree that there are five broad factors underlying personality, and these are typically referred to as the 'big five' factors of personality. They are:

- Extroversion – if you score highly on this scale you may be the sort of person who is described as sociable, warm or assertive.
- Neuroticism – scoring highly on this scale would probably mean that you are the sort of person who is often described as anxious, self-conscious or impulsive.
- Openness to experience – a high score here means that you are likely to be open to new ideas, artistic or creative.
- Agreeableness – a high score here means that you are trusting, kind or modest.
- Conscientiousness – scoring highly on this scale would probably mean that you are organized, reliable or that you strive for achievement.

Some personality questionnaires are designed to measure the 'big five' factors directly, whereas others are designed to measure narrower factors. Whether a questionnaire measures broad or narrow factors depends on the level of detail in which recruiters are interested, and this is not something you need be concerned about.

Is there an ideal personality profile?

The answer is 'no'. Some people can consider one personality characteristic desirable, while others regard the same characteristic as undesirable. Similarly in the workplace, some personality characteristics are considered beneficial for certain occupations but not for others. For example, extroversion is a characteristic that is beneficial in a sales job but not in a job that includes routine activities. There is no universal profile that companies are looking for when they are recruiting. Each company will look for profiles with characteristics that are suitable for each job.

Can you make your profile look more desirable?

Companies that use personality questionnaires for selection will typically look at the match between your personality profile and the characteristics that are considered beneficial for the specific role. In theory, therefore, you could make your profile look more desirable, but there are two points you need to consider.

First, do you actually want to make your profile look more desirable? You should bear in mind that if your personality doesn't match the job, this will also mean that the job will not match your personality. Do you really want to get a job that you might find boring, stressful, frustrating or hard to cope with?

Second, can you really make your profile look more desirable? You might think that this would be an easy thing to do and might be tempted to try it. However, I should warn you that it is not. You must understand that companies decide which personality profile is suitable for a position through a process known as job analysis. This involves researching scientific literature, shadowing current employees and interviewing them (and also their managers) to develop an understanding of what tasks the job involves. When these tasks have been identified, the personality factors that would be required to perform these tasks successfully need to be identified as well. For example, if a job involves proof-reading documents, one personality characteristic that would be required is 'attention to detail'. This is a narrow personality characteristic that falls under the broader factor of conscientiousness. Recruiters might be looking for people who are high on 'attention to detail' or for people who are high on 'conscientiousness'.

At this point you might think that you could identify the basic personality characteristics required by a job role by using logic. Of course, if it were as easy as this, companies would not pay qualified consultants to do the job, but let us imagine that you are indeed able to identify the required personality characteristics. What would you have to do next? The psychologist or consultant who identifies the desired personality characteristics has to set limits on 'how much' of each characteristic an applicant needs to possess. So even if you could deduce the characteristics that are important for a role, you would also need to estimate how high your score would have to be for each characteristic.

To take this one step further, let's say that you could indeed accurately estimate what recruiters are looking for. You would then need to know how to answer each question on the questionnaire in order to achieve the desired score. This is not something that you can simply estimate, however. Remember that your scores are actually compared to a group of individuals to show how 'high' or 'low' you are on each personality factor. Therefore, to know which score is considered high, you would also need to know how the people in the comparison group have responded.

Ultimately, therefore, there are so many things that you might estimate wrongly that it is just not a good idea to try. In trying to show a more desirable personality profile, you might end up showing something that doesn't really match what the company is looking for, when in reality you could be ideal for the job. Although in theory you could make your profile look more desirable, this is both hard to do and quite risky. Even if you could do it, it would not be to your benefit in the long run.

Sample personality questionnaire

You can see overleaf what a personality questionnaire might look like. This is an example of a personality questionnaire with adjectives rather than questions, and it was designed especially for this book, so its reliability and validity have not been tested. However, data are available from a comparison group, which means that your scores can actually mean something rather than just being a number. You will be able to see broadly where you lie on each personality scale.

In addition to finding out what your personality profile might look like, there are several other advantages in completing the personality questionnaire. First, you will get a better understanding of the 'big five' factors, and when you complete a questionnaire as part of a selection process you will have some idea of what the questions you answer are measuring. You will also get a better understanding of how a personality questionnaire is scored. Moreover, completing it will make you familiar with the format of the questionnaire, and you will be less anxious about facing something that is unknown.

To find out what your profile might look like, read the instructions below on how to complete the questionnaire, and respond to each adjective as honestly as possible. Remember that there are no right or wrong answers in personality questionnaires.

Personality questionnaire

This questionnaire is composed of a list of 60 adjectives. Please respond to each of the adjectives and indicate the extent to which you feel that each applies to you, using the 1 to 5 response scale below.

I believe this adjective or phrase to be true of me:

1.	Never	Circle number 1
2.	Rarely	Circle number 2
3.	Sometimes/Occasionally	Circle number 3
4.	Often/Generally	Circle number 4
5.	Always	Circle number 5

1. Talkative
   (1) (2) (3) (4) (5)
2. Doubting
   (1) (2) (3) (4) (5)
3. Methodical
   (1) (2) (3) (4) (5)
4. Anxious
   (1) (2) (3) (4) (5)
5. Imaginative
   (1) (2) (3) (4) (5)
6. Private
   (1) (2) (3) (4) (5)
7. Modest
   (1) (2) (3) (4) (5)
8. Unstructured
   (1) (2) (3) (4) (5)
9. Confident
   (1) (2) (3) (4) (5)
10. Conservative
    (1) (2) (3) (4) (5)

11. Friendly
    (1) (2) (3) (4) (5)
12. Suspicious
    (1) (2) (3) (4) (5)
13. Tidy
    (1) (2) (3) (4) (5)
14. Nervous
    (1) (2) (3) (4) (5)
15. Creative
    (1) (2) (3) (4) (5)
16. Reserved
    (1) (2) (3) (4) (5)
17. Trusting
    (1) (2) (3) (4) (5)
18. Impulsive
    (1) (2) (3) (4) (5)
19. Optimistic
    (1) (2) (3) (4) (5)
20. Conventional
    (1) (2) (3) (4) (5)

21. Outgoing
    (1) (2) (3) (4) (5)
22. Tough-minded
    (1) (2) (3) (4) (5)
23. Organized
    (1) (2) (3) (4) (5)
24. Angry
    (1) (2) (3) (4) (5)
25. Original
    (1) (2) (3) (4) (5)
26. Shy
    (1) (2) (3) (4) (5)
27. Sympathetic
    (1) (2) (3) (4) (5)
28. Risk-taking
    (1) (2) (3) (4) (5)
29. Enthusiastic
    (1) (2) (3) (4) (5)
30. Traditional
    (1) (2) (3) (4) (5)

For each row, add the five numbers that you have indicated and enter the total in the box at the end of that row (Box E1 to O2).

To calculate your score on each personality factor, enter the totals from boxes E1 to O2 in the appropriate boxes below and make the computations indicated:

Extroversion $E1$ − $E2$ =

Agreeableness $A2$ − $A1$ =

Conscientiousness $C1$ − $C2$ =

Neuroticism $N1$ − $N2$ =

Openness $O1$ − $O2$ =

31. Assertive
① ② ③ ④ ⑤

32. Wary
① ② ③ ④ ⑤

33. Dutiful
① ② ③ ④ ⑤

34. Depressed
① ② ③ ④ ⑤

35. Inquisitive
① ② ③ ④ ⑤

36. Quiet
① ② ③ ④ ⑤

37. Caring
① ② ③ ④ ⑤

38. Spontaneous
① ② ③ ④ ⑤

39. Calm
① ② ③ ④ ⑤

40. Conforming
① ② ③ ④ ⑤

41. Cheerful
① ② ③ ④ ⑤

42. Judgemental
① ② ③ ④ ⑤

43. Disciplined
① ② ③ ④ ⑤

44. Stressed
① ② ③ ④ ⑤

45. Innovative
① ② ③ ④ ⑤

46. Secretive
① ② ③ ④ ⑤

47. Kind
① ② ③ ④ ⑤

48. Unplanned
① ② ③ ④ ⑤

49. Positive
① ② ③ ④ ⑤

50. Cautious
① ② ③ ④ ⑤

E1

A1

C1

N1

O1

E2

A2

C2

N2

O2

With the scores from the personality questionnaire it is possible to indicate work environments that might suit your personality. The following pointers are work environments that seem to reflect your responses. Remember that this is just a general guide and that your choice of career or particular job will be influenced by a lot more than these results.

Three sets of pointers are outlined for each scale, and each set relates to a different range of scores. Find your score on each scale but note the relevant pointers.

You are likely to prefer and be better suited to work environments

Extroversion

SCORE	DESCRIPTION
−20 to 0	• Where you can be somewhat more reserved when dealing with the public or colleagues • Where you can take a more low-profile role • Where you are not required to take a public stance on issues
1 to 9	• Where there is a balance between working with others and working alone
10 to 20	• Where you can be sociable and enthusiastic • Where you have the opportunity to work with lots of others • Where there is contact with the public

Agreeableness

SCORE	DESCRIPTION
–20 to –1	• Where open, frank speaking is preferred • Where there is some need to confront issues openly and people will not be easily offended • Where your own needs and the needs of the organization are considered paramount • Where difficult decisions need to be made • Where decisions are highly political or contentious
0 to 12	• Where tactfulness is balanced with some frank discussion when necessary • Where there must be a balance between reaching a goal and considering the effects on other people
13 to 20	• Where tolerance and consideration of others are required • Where issues need to be dealt with sensitively • Where other people are put first • Where you do not need to take or implement decisions that adversely affect others • Where decisions are not highly political or contentious

Conscientiousness

SCORE	DESCRIPTION
−20 to −1	• Where a relatively casual approach to order and tidiness is the norm • Where the 'big picture' is considered more important than the detail • Where self-imposed order is not a major factor • Where there is access to administrative or secretarial support
0 to 11	• Where a degree of planning and organizing is required • Where accuracy and attention to detail are important but not essential • Where you will not feel dominated by over-messy or over-fastidious colleagues
12 to 20	• Where a high level of organizational skills is required • Where self-discipline and a structured approach are important • Where accuracy and attention to detail are definite assets • Where things need to be planned and prioritized • Where things need to be kept neat and tidy

Neuroticism

SCORE	DESCRIPTION
−20 to −10	• Where high levels of self-confidence are required • Where it may be necessary to cope with high levels of pressure or stress • Where you can feel regularly challenged • Where you can actively seek responsibility
−9 to 2	• Where you feel comfortable with the requirements of the job • Where some self-confidence is needed but colleagues can be called on in times of need
3 to 20	• Where a degree of caution may be required • Where you need to be careful, such as in safety-critical or highly regulated environments • Where you are not required to make major decisions • Where you will not be exposed to high degrees of stress or pressure

Openness

SCORE	DESCRIPTION
−20 to −1	• Where there are clear and established rules and procedures • Where a more conventional and traditional approach to work is preferred • Where tried and trusted methods are preferred
0 to 9	• Where it is possible to strike a balance between conventionality and individualism • Where tried and trusted methods are considered as valuable as the new and innovative • Where creativity is encouraged but not always required
10 to 20	• Where people are encouraged to express their individuality • Where the workplace is free of formal structure and convention • Where you will have the opportunity to try out new ideas, use your imagination and think creatively

Further reading

I hope I have been able to demystify psychometric tests by explaining the thinking behind them and giving you an insight into how the questions are constructed. You should now feel confident that, with a bit of practice and preparation, you can face any test and perform to the best of your abilities. If you would like to try a few more sample questions or would like to have a go at filling out tests online, here are a few websites you could try:

http://www.kenexa.com
http://www.morrisby.com
http://www.shldirect.com/shldirect-homepage/SHLDirect-1.asp
http://www.psychometrics-uk.com/bapt.html
http://www.mensa.org/workout2.php
http://www.ets.org/
http://www.psychometric-success.com/
http://www.savilleconsulting.com/
http://www.assessmentday.co.uk/

If you would like more specific information on types of psychometric tests, I recommend:

Joanna Moutafi and Ian Newcombe, *Perfect Numerical Test Results* (London, Random House, 2007)
Helen Baron, *Perfect Personality Profiles* (London, Random House, 2007)

And if you're looking for more general information on applying for jobs, you could try:

Max Eggert, *Perfect Interview* (London, Random House, 2003)

Max Eggert, *Perfect Answers to Interview Questions* (London, Random House, 2005)

Max Eggert, *Perfect CV* (London, Random House, 2003)

Answers to practice questions

Numerical reasoning tests

Question	Answer
Simple calculations	
1.	23
2.	31
3.	59
4.	5
5.	29
6.	13
7.	35
8.	11
9.	39
10.	56
11.	54
12.	72
13.	6
14.	9
15.	13
16.	12
17.	9
18.	5
Rounding off	
19.	13.45
20.	10.22
21.	29.2
22.	35.9

Question	Answer
23.	1
25.	2.2
Averages	
26.	14.8
27.	396.7
28.	0.2
29.	16.7
30.	1.9
31.	30.4
Percentages	
32.	0.13
33.	0.76
34.	0.18
35.	0.209
36.	0.856
37.	0.989
38.	28.7%
39.	45.6%
40.	240.5%
41.	40
42.	52.5
43.	240
44.	£3.60

Question	Answer
45.	135
46.	195
47.	25%
48.	20%
49.	52.90%
50.	29.30%
51.	7.50%
52.	53.30%
53.	3,125
54.	448
55.	1,125
56.	18°C
57.	5,150,000
58.	£34,500
59.	£1,064,800
60.	75
61.	212,5
62.	1,950,000
63.	120
64.	3,825
65.	322
66.	7.14%
67.	120%
68.	16.67%
69.	6.06%
70.	25%
71.	24%
72.	37.50%
73.	40%
74.	42.86%
75.	3.53%
76.	40%
77.	12.5%

Question	Answer
Ratios	
78.	04:01
79.	0.25:1
80.	0.83:1
81.	1.1:1
82.	0.19:1
83.	2.5:1
84.	40
85.	72
86.	80.67
87.	4
88.	21
89.	30
90.	20
91.	75
92.	60
93.	201,005
94.	337,500
95.	350,000
Tables	
96.	900
97.	440
98.	0.24
99.	0.41
100.	1.3:1
101.	800
102.	1,425
103.	d
104.	b
105.	c
106.	a
107.	b

Question	Answer		Question	Answer
108.	e		133.	d
109.	e		134.	a
110.	e		135.	b
			136.	c
Bar charts			137.	e
111.	d		138.	d
112.	b		139.	c
113.	c		140.	b
114.	b		141.	d
115.	c		142.	e
116.	e		143.	b
117.	c		144.	c
118.	a		145.	d
119.	b		146.	a
120.	c		147.	a
			148.	e
Graphs			149.	c
121.	a		150.	e
122.	d			
123.	e		**Non-graphical**	
124.	b		151.	c
125.	d		152.	d
			153.	d
Pie charts			154.	b
126.	d		155.	d
127.	e		156.	c
128.	b		157.	d
129.	c		158.	e
130.	a		159.	a
			160.	e
Sequences			161.	b
131.	c		162.	c
132.	d		163.	d

Question	Answer
164.	c
165.	d

Verbal reasoning tests

Spelling test 1

Question	Answer
166.	c
167.	a
168.	b
169.	c
170.	a
171.	b
172.	c
173.	c
174.	b
175.	a
176.	c
177.	b
178.	c
179.	a
180.	c
181.	b
182.	a
183.	b

Spelling test 2

Question	Answer
184.	a
185.	b
186.	b
187.	a
188.	a

Question	Answer
189.	a
190.	b
191.	c
192.	a
193.	c
194.	a
195.	b
196.	c
197.	a
198.	b
199.	a
200.	c
201.	b
202.	a
203.	c

Word comprehension

Question	Answer
204.	a
205.	b
206.	a
207.	c
208.	a
209.	b
210.	c
211.	a
212.	b
213.	c
214.	a
215.	a
216.	c
217.	b
218.	b
219.	a

Question	Answer
220.	c
221.	b
222.	c
223.	a

Word analogies 1

Question	Answer
224.	a
225.	b
226.	c
227.	d
228.	b
229.	a
230.	b
231.	e
232.	b
233.	c
234.	d
235.	e
236.	b
237.	b
238.	d
239.	c
240.	c
241.	c
242.	d

Question	Answer
243.	a
244.	d

Word analogies 2

Question	Answer
245.	d
246.	d
247.	c
248.	b
249.	c
250.	c
251.	d
252.	a
253.	e
254.	e
255.	c
256.	e
257.	c
258.	b
259.	d
260.	c
261.	e
262.	d
263.	b
264.	e

Text comprehension: true, false and 'Cannot Say' questions

Q	A	Explanation
265.	CS	The text states that the action of these cells is perfectly balanced but makes no mention of their numbers.
266.	F	Osteoporosis is due to less bone being replenished than degraded.
267.	CS	The text does not specify the causes of osteoporosis.
268.	CS	This is not stated in the text.
269.	F	The research team has only linked drug addiction to genes.
270.	CS	The receptors are not increased; they are made more vulnerable by the genetic variation.
271.	T	This can be deduced from the second and third sentences.
272.	CS	This is an outcome of the research, not necessarily its purpose; no information is provided on the purpose of the research.
273.	CS	It is stated that one of the factors is no more than light winds. This implies that strong winds may prevent cyclones from forming, but it does not logically follow that no wind would do the same.
274.	T	This can be inferred from the third sentence.
275.	CS	Their beneficial and destructive effects are not directly compared.
276.	F	It moves heat to higher latitudes.
277.	F	The brain causes the airway muscles to be activated when it senses the build-up of carbon dioxide.
278.	CS	This is not explicitly stated in the text.
279.	CS	This is not specified in the text.
280.	T	The text states that initial research showed no benefits.
281.	CS	This is not stated in the text.
282.	T	This can be inferred from the first and second sentences.
283.	F	This is stated as the principal technique; therefore it cannot be the only one.

Q	A	Explanation
284.	CS	It is not stated that they had not been investigated earlier.
285.	T	The total amount of interest is the same as a normal deposit account, but it is shared among a few lucky winners. Therefore, most people will not win and will receive less interest.
286.	F	The lottery does not affect the value of the deposit.
287.	F	The total amount of interest is the same as in a normal deposit account.
288.	CS	The interest is shared among a lucky few, but there is no indication whether the probable winnings would equal the normal interest or not.
289.	T	This can be inferred from the first sentence.
290.	CS	The text mentions only proportions, not actual numbers.
291.	F	The text mentions 36 months of falling unemployment throughout the UK.
292.	T	This can be inferred from the last sentence.
293.	F	Inflation helps borrowers at the expense of lenders.
294.	CS	It may have similar effects, but it is not necessarily the same.
295.	F	The public sector is a net borrower, whereas the private sector is a net lender.
296.	T	This is paraphrasing the third sentence.
297.	T	Its three purposes are to notify the fire department, to sound alarm bells and to shut down the air-handling units.
298.	T	It is better to have the fire department respond and not be needed than to have them arrive too late for potential rescue.
299.	F	You should use the correct type of fire extinguisher, not the first one you find.
300.	CS	Although the text states that it is preferable to have a false alarm rather than delay calling the fire department,

Q	A	Explanation
		there is nothing in the text about the attitude of the fire department to false alarms.
301.	T	If a record number of grants was made in 2006, it implies that there were fewer in other years.
302.	F	Only 15 per cent of 2006 awards were to sub-Saharan Africa students.
303.	CS	No information is provided on the students that receive grants.
304.	CS	This is not stated in the text.
305.	F	Tissa was her husband's successor not her husband.
306.	CS	The passage gives no information about the number of people who were Buddhists in Sri Lanka.
307.	CS	The passage states that she is the earliest known female monarch in Asia, but there could have been an earlier one in other continents.
308.	T	She poisoned her husband and her husband's successor.
309.	T	These deposits preserve more than the usual geological record so allow us to have greater information on what lifeforms existed at that time.
310.	CS	The absence of oxygen reduces the activity of bacteria, but we do not actually know the cause of death.
311.	F	Archeopteryx is an example of how knoservat-lagerstätten help preserve the softer parts of ancient organisms.
312.	F	The passage suggests that aquatic lifeforms benefit most, but as archaeopteryx, which is a bird, has also been preserved, it is not exclusive to aquatic animals.
313.	F	A simple majority of the people who have voted in the referendum is required.
314.	CS	Although the president cannot veto an amendment, this does not mean that no president has ever disagreed.
315.	F	The passage states that UK citizens can vote in general elections.

Q	A	Explanation
316.	T	The first sentence says that it must be adopted by the Dáil and Senate first, and the second sentence says it must be endorsed by the electorate.
317.	F	It is implied that they did end with the death of the losers as the gladiatorial games are described in this fashion by way of contrast.
318.	T	The passage mentions 'greater resources' and 'these spectacles were reserved for exceptional occasions'.
319.	CS	It is possible, but we are given one example with these figures rather than a general guide on the number of people involved.
320.	CS	There is no link made in the passage between them, but it might be possible.
321.	CS	The passage refers to a bee as 'her' but we don't know from the passage the incidence of males to females in honeybees.
322.	T	Because humans are mammals, and the stinger will become lodged in their skin.
323.	F	The stinger evolved for inter-bee combat.
324.	CS	No information is provided on the frequency with which bees sting mammals.
325.	F	They are not equipped for cold temperatures like the Bactrian camels.
326.	F	Dromedary camels have a short fibre coat, even in winter.
327.	CS	They are not native there, but we do not know their prevalence.
328.	T	These are Bactrian camels.
329.	F	They are placed between the knees and played with the fingers.
330.	T	This can be inferred from the last sentence.
331.	T	They can be traced back to the nineteenth century.
332.	F	They do exist but mainly with ceramic bodies.

Q	A	Explanation
333.	T	The London Underground was the first, and it started in 1863.
334.	T	The second sentence states that 55 per cent of the system is above ground.
335.	CS	There are 3 million passenger journeys, but many of these might be return journeys by the same people.
336.	F	This is the distance run by trains in the year 2004–2005.
337.	T	He was born in 1898 in the Netherlands.
338.	F	He published this in the 'later years', when he had left Italy.
339.	F	In 1922 he would have been at least 23.
340.	T	Although this is likely, it is not explicitly stated in the text.
341.	T	A small tricorn hat and a fashionable eighteenth-century male.
342.	F	The term was introduced in the eighteenth century.
343.	F	*Maccherone* is Italian for boorish fool.
344.	F	It is a small hat.

Text comprehension: multiple choice questions

Q	A	Explanation
345.	CS	The text states that in some variants males have a large bump on the beak, but this may not be the case for all types of Swan Goose.
	CS	No information is given in the text about why the Swan Goose is so named.
	CS	Although natural breeding grounds are now in Mongolia, it is not stated whether historically this is the region of origin.

Q	A	Explanation
	d	T	The Swan Goose has been domesticated in south and east China for centuries.
346.		CS	No information is given regarding alternative routes other than from Leh.
		CS	No information is provided on the ranking of Pangong's altitude.
	c	T	The text states that most of the lake's length falls within Chinese territory.
		CS	The text implies that salt water lakes are unlikely to freeze.
347.	a	T	Sleep loss is linked to obesity through metabolic changes and reduced exercise.
		CS	The text states that the findings are based on a review of existing research.
		CS	The text does not provide any comparison of the relative effects of sleep loss on children and adolescents.
		CS	The text states only tentatively that changes in body mechanisms may contribute to diabetes.
348.	a	T	Smenkhkare was Akhenaten's successor, so would have been alive during his reign.
		CS	The text states only that this is opinion.
		CS	The text states that this is only a possibility.
		CS	Tutankhamun may have ruled during the Eighteenth Dynasty, but no information is given as to how many rulers preceded him.
349.		CS	The text does not mention when Cleopatra ruled Egypt.
		F	Hieroglyphics were added after 200 years.
		CS	The text does not state whether the inscriptions are identical on all three obelisks.
	d	T	The text states that the 'Needles' are a trio of obelisks.

Q	A	Explanation
350.		CS	Information is provided only about the leading national companies, not all companies or overall advertising expenditure.
		CS	The text reports a common belief; however, it is not clear whether this is for most leading national advertisers.
	c	T	The text states that advertising efficiency is difficult to measure.
		CS	It is not clear from the text that increased advertising leads to more sales.
351.		CS	According to the passage this is a possibility, not a definite outcome.
		CS	This is not stated in the text.
		CS	Only its effect on warm-blooded creatures is mentioned, but it is not explicitly stated that this is the only case.
	d	T	This can be inferred from the last three sentences.
352.		CS	The traditional approach focused on the production of goods.
		CS	Although both have an interest, no information is provided about which is greater.
	c	T	The text links the growth of 'consumer society' to this area of economics.
		CS	Although consumer economics has become important, it is not stated whether this is the case within the last ten years.
353.		F	Inductive reasoning that is based on observation is not a valid method of proof.
		CS	Inductive reasoning is useful for generating hypotheses, but no information on its importance is provided.
	c	T	Inductive reasoning is not a valid method of proof, hence valid methods would not require this.

Q	A		Explanation
		CS	No information is provided about the efficacy of inductive reasoning for dealing with simple situations.
354.		CS	No information is provided that the blue iguana is not found elsewhere.
		F	The iguanas are not released until they are large enough to survive being eaten by snakes.
		F	The iguana population decrease is the result of habitat loss.
	d	T	This can be inferred from the third sentence.
355.		CS	The passage does not state where this is exactly in relation to London Bridge.
		F	There is a London Bridge in Arizona, but not the original one, as there have been five bridges at the site.
	c	T	It was opened in 1973.
		CS	There is no mention of its current value.
356.		F	They weigh less than 220 kilograms.
		CS	They may eat other things that are not mentioned.
		F	White tigers are a colour variation of Bengal tigers.
	d	T	The size of their territory varies according to the availability of prey.
357.		F	The text states that the amphitheatre in El Djem remained intact until the seventeenth century, not that it was still used for sports and games.
		CS	The passage states only that El Djem is one of these, but there is no mention of the Colosseum.
	c	T	The largest is in Rome and this could seat only up to 50,000.
		F	It is located in Rome, Italy.
358.	a	T	The counterweight balances the weight of the bridge like a seesaw.
		F	It used to, but it is now powered by oil and electricity.
		CS	They are the most common movable bridge in existence, not necessarily of any type of bridge.

Q	A	Explanation
		CS	Although this is likely, the passage mentions only the upwards swing.
359.		CS	The passage mentions only that pruning must be done in the proper season.
		F	The wires are used for shaping.
		CS	There is no mention of this in the passage.
	d	T	This can be inferred from the fourth sentence.
360.		CS	The 24-monthly term means that this may not be the case if the permanent members also take a turn in being president.
		CS	The text does not mention whether the temporary members can veto resolutions at all.
	c	T	This is how the UN Security Council differs from the other organizations of the UN.
		F	Only the temporary members are voted in.
361.	a	T	The resin is allowed to harden before being extracted.
		F	Omani frankincense is the best quality so it will be opaque.
		CS	The time may not be evenly spread across the years; the information provided is not clear on this.
		CS	This is possible, but it is not stated in the passage.
362.		CS	It is unique in having five languages used; we don't know about lower numbers than that.
		CS	This is possible, but it is not stated in the text.
	c	T	The text states that some anthems are merely fanfares so they are not sung.
		CS	There is not sufficient information to infer how many anthems there were outside Europe.
363.		F	It can be inferred that they are designed to scare children, but not to terrify them.
		CS	This is not mentioned at all.
		CS	This could be true, but it is not mentioned in the passage.

Q	A		Explanation
	d	T	There are lots of 'typically' and 'usually', which suggests that there are some variations.
364.		F	Armour was decorated with the same basic principle, not with etching.
	b	T	The first etchings date from the sixteenth century, well after the period of the Ancient Romans.
		CS	Three of the four artists mentioned are German or Dutch, but this is hardly a universal truth.
		CS	It comes from drawing in the same way as with pen or pencil on paper but isn't necessarily produced with these.

Abstract reasoning tests

Question	Answer		Question	Answer
365.	c		382.	c
366.	b		383.	e
367.	d		384.	b
368.	b		385.	e
369.	c		386.	c
370.	b		387.	c
371.	b		388.	b
372.	e		389.	a
373.	a		390.	d
374.	e		391.	e
375.	d		392.	d
376.	e		393.	d
377.	b		394.	b
378.	a		395.	a
379.	b		396.	b
380.	e		397.	c
381.	c		398.	e

Question	Answer		Question	Answer
399.	e		402.	a
400.	d		403.	b
401.	a		404.	d

Order more titles in the *Perfect* series
from your local bookshop, or have them delivered
direct to your door by Bookpost.

☐ Perfect Answers to Interview Questions	Max Eggert	9781905211722	£7.99
☐ Perfect Babies' Names	Rosalind Fergusson	9781905211661	£5.99
☐ Perfect Best Man	George Davidson	9781905211784	£5.99
☐ Perfect CV	Max Eggert	9781905211739	£7.99
☐ Perfect Interview	Max Eggert	9781905211746	£7.99
☐ Perfect Numerical Test Results	Joanna Moutafi and Ian Newcombe	9781905211333	£7.99
☐ Perfect Personality Profiles	Helen Baron	9781905211821	£7.99
☐ Perfect Pub Quiz	David Pickering	9781905211692	£6.99
☐ Perfect Punctuation	Stephen Curtis	9781905211685	£5.99
☐ Perfect Readings for Weddings	Jonathan Law	9781905211098	£6.99
☐ Perfect Wedding Speeches and Toasts	George Davidson	9781905211777	£5.99

Free post and packing
Overseas customers allow £2 per paperback

Phone: 01624 677237

Post: Random House Books
c/o Bookpost, PO Box 29, Douglas, Isle of Man IM99 1BQ

Fax: 01624 670 923

email: bookshop@enterprise.net

Cheques (payable to Bookpost) and credit cards accepted

Prices and availability subject to change without notice.
Allow 28 days for delivery.
When placing your order, please state if you do not
wish to receive any additional information.

www.randomhouse.co.uk